11 PERSONAL ESSAYS ABOUT OVERCOMING TRAUMA

Women Therapists on Healing

SUSAN PEASE BANITT, LCSW
& LARISSA MIRANDA

Helping talented writers publish exceptional books

This is a work of essays. It reflects numerous recollections
of experiences over time. Some names may have been changed to
protect privacy, some events have been compressed, and
some dialogue has been recreated.

Praise for Women Therapists on Healing

"Eleven trauma experts come together in this book to share the personal journeys that led them to developing innovative and effective ways of treating trauma. We don't often see this, because most known trauma experts are men, and men don't usually share in this manner. These experts are women. The diversity of their experiences, of the kinds of trauma they treat, and their approaches have much to teach all of us who struggle to understand and help our traumatized clients. If you don't know these experts yet, you should."

— Alison Miller, retired psychologist, author of *Demystifying Mind Control and Ritual Abuse*, *Healing the Unimaginable*, and *Becoming Yourself*

"*Women Therapists on Healing* not only serves as a testament to the humanness of healers but also acts as a valuable resource for anyone seeking a deeper understanding of trauma and its impact. This book delves into the multifaceted aspects of trauma and the healers who treat it, while shedding light on the often-overlooked struggles faced by underrepresented communities. *Women Therapists on Healing* will make a significant contribution to the field, fostering greater awareness and compassion for those working in the mental health profession and the people they treat."

— Jaime Pollack, founder and director of community engagement for An Infinite Mind

"*Women Therapists on Healing* invites us to heal holistically by drawing from the lived body wisdom of each woman and story. These women are poets and healers who have shared their breathtaking wisdom filled with magic, light, and a soothing balm that is being offered as a gift to other survivors. This anthology can gently guide Black women, femmes, and nonbinary survivors of trauma to explore the impact of trauma on the mind, body, heart, and spirit. It was truly an honor to be allowed into the sacred space of these powerful women who share their journey with us on how trauma has impacted their lives and the lives of their loved ones. Many survivors will immediately see themselves in the pages of this anthology, while others will find themselves."

— Michelle Lewis, MSW, CSWA, SWP,
owner of Third Eye Books, Accessories & Gifts
and Third Eye Wholistic Wellness

Contents

Part Three
Life-Threatening Events and Healthcare Systems

Introduction

How do women heal? How do we endure the myriad of traumas life throws at us? How do we overcome when the odds are not in our favor? I have contemplated these questions for decades as a woman, a therapist, and a survivor of unspeakable early childhood trauma. My way of healing was to help others heal. My way of healing others was to heal myself. As a classically trained psychiatric social worker, I keep clear boundaries between my personal self and my professional self. None of my patients know my personal story, but they know I have suffered trauma. This knowledge helps them feel safe enough to open up and trust that I will not belittle their symptoms or challenge their stories. They perceive my healing journey even if it is not articulated in a session. And so it is with all the authors in this book. They, too, have suffered. They, too, are boundaried professionals. They, too, wish to heal and be healed.

This book was born in a strike of lightning. In June 2021, I was catching up on my CEUs (continuing education units, required for licensure) during a weekend workshop with a popular author and trauma expert, a man who shall remain unnamed. Over the course of two days, he mentioned several trauma experts by name, perhaps seven to eight people. All but one (an expert he could not avoid mentioning) were men. I even asked a question in the chat thread, addressing this bias. It was ignored. He continually referenced the same names I have been hearing for more than twenty-five years. A familiar feeling of irritation, then despair, then rage swept over me. All my career, which spans nearly fifty years, men have talked about other men in the field. They rarely mention women, and if so, only a token woman, the one outstanding difference contrasting against all the lionized male figures. I realized that not once, in all my decades of practice, had I heard a man introduce and uplift a woman in the field who was doing amazing work. Not once had I heard a man spontaneously cite his inspiration from a female mentor, author, student, or therapist that he had not been forced to mention. Not. One. Time. It was the worst kind of "aha moment." Male experts, I realized, do not pass the baton to women.

I thought about all the women who seek therapy from other women, how women comprise the vast majority of therapy clients, and how women provide the vast majority of therapy around the world. I thought about how, over the years, I only see one man in my office or in my trauma classes for every seven women I see—and how that number has remained stable over time. I thought about how many times women's practices and papers have inspired men, men who never bothered to mention these women's names but claimed the information as if they, themselves, had discovered it. I flashed on all the amazing women authors and trauma experts I have met over the years, some of whom have become dear personal friends, none of whom are as widely known as these men, despite years of teaching, despite their numerous journal articles and books published. So, I called on them and said, "Wanna write a book with me?" They all said, "Yes!" *Women Therapists on Healing* was born in that uncomfortable realization that we need a compilation of healing strategies, tools, and stories written by and for women.

"Wild Geese," the popular poem by the late Mary Oliver, embodies acceptance of this migration to peace that we undertake when we engage our healing process fully. The poem is filled with acceptance: acceptance of the journey, acceptance of who and what we love, acceptance of the rhythm of nature, acceptance of the passage and cycles of time. Acceptance is a burden at first, and then a balm for healing trauma. We move through many different landscapes on that passage: sun, "pebbles of rain," trees, prairies, mountains, and rivers, heading home. Oliver acknowledges our loneliness and our connection. She gives us permission to fully inhabit our bodies and to let go of judgment or the need for repentance for just being or for having suffered. Like the geese calling, we are called back into relationship, into "the family of things."

"Tell me about your despair, yours, and I will tell you about mine." This is how women have healed from time out of mind. In the kitchen, in a coffee shop, in a women's circle, we tell each other our stories. The telling of stories elicits more stories. The natural rhythm of deep sharing isn't question and answer, it is mutual disclosure in a field of deep listening, acceptance, and nonjudgment. I asked the authors to share some of their own journey along with their wisdom because women's suffering is universal. There is no "them"; there is only "us."

In the therapy hour, we have been necessarily, if uncomfortably, restricted to keep our stories to ourselves. We get paid for this service; it is our job and our honor. The benefit, of course, is an hour totally focused on the client's needs and stories. There is a cost, too. Therapists get into a habit of suppressing our stories. We can feel excluded from the circle of healing. Or we can develop a false view of ourselves, as therapists who are "above it all." Every therapist is a human being with suffering. We do not become therapists because we have problems. Everyone has problems. We become therapists because we want to be part of the solution.

I wanted this book to reflect the diversity of women therapists and their experiences. Various authors of this book identify as Christian, Jewish, Indigenous, Spiritual, Celtic, Black, African American, Biracial, Mestiza, and Maori. We are from the USA, Canada, and Australia. Many of us fall into the LGBTQ+ collective. We struggle at times with our own traumas, secondary traumas from our work, physical disabilities, and chronic invisible illnesses. Many of us have abuse histories. All of us have experienced multiple levels of oppression within our fields and in our lives, and many of us have internalized that at some point as "imposter syndrome." Some of us work with individuals; others with groups or systems. Some of these authors are quite well-known as leaders and influencers in their circles, and some are emerging.

As you read these very frank chapters, you may find yourself becoming activated or even triggered. *I have not posted trigger warnings, because each chapter has material that some portion of readers may find overwhelming—others will find the same material comforting.* Go slowly and mindfully through this book. Engage in self-care as you read. Pause often. Do not push yourself. Allow yourself to be drawn to whatever you need in this book. And drink a lot of water in case your body/mind detoxes while it absorbs new information.

Like geese, women's ways of leading are different from men's. Geese fly in a formation where everyone can see everyone else. When the leader gets tired, they drop back, and a more energized bird takes the lead. The flock is egalitarian and functions on a basis of empathy. I hope you enjoy this compilation of our "wild geese," women leaders who are here to lead and be led, to share and be shared with. They embody diversity, have many stories to tell, and much wisdom to share.

Blessings and healing to all,
Susan Pease Banitt, LCSW

Part One

Dissociation and Remembering

Chapter 1

Did That Really Happen to Me? Evidence and Remembering in Healing Trauma

Susan Pease Banitt, LCSW

I sat on the sofa across from my therapist. My mind felt as though it was splitting open. It was a disturbing sensation, like standing on thin ice on a cracking lake as the temperature warmed—dangerous and unstable. Shannon was calmly alert, holding me with his gaze. An hour earlier I had called him, feeling like I was losing my mind; I couldn't function at all. He had invited me to an emergency session. I had five-year-old twins at home and needed to wait for my husband to relieve me. I got there as soon as I could.

"What is your worst fear?" he asked.

I hesitated, afraid of what would come out of my mouth. He waited patiently.

"I'm afraid ___ molested me." I felt nothing.

He continued to hold me with his stolid presence. "Say it again."

I took a deep breath. "I'm afraid ___ molested me."

All of a sudden, my body flooded with the knowledge of the truth of what I had just said. Every cell knew. The sensation was as if gallons of mud had been dumped into a utility sink with a drain too small. My body felt leaden and weary. My mind surrendered its disbelief. *Shit*, I thought. *Shit!* What I know now that I didn't know then is that I had encountered a true narrative memory fragment.

It would take years to unpack that realization and reassociate the profoundly disturbing memories from earliest childhood—horrible but necessary work, as is all trauma therapy. Was it worth it? Yes! My PTSD completely resolved, as did my generalized anxiety disorder, which I now consider a prodromal form of PTSD, much like the pain people get before a herpes blister manifests and opens up for healing. I do not share my traumatic memories, however, with any but the closest of friends and family because I am aware that although they have ceased to be traumatic to me, they may be traumatic to a reader.

Remembering

Remembering is a necessary part of healing. Judith Herman, in her famous book *Trauma and Recovery: The Aftermath of Violence—From Domestic Abuse to Political Terror* (2020), labeled it the second of three stages of healing from trauma. People often say, "Don't live in the past!" Fully processing memories, paradoxically, is the only way to fully live in the present. Freud famously said, "Whatever is not acknowledged or remembered is destined to be acted out." I would add, "Whatever is not acknowledged or remembered is destined to make you suffer forever in your body/mind." When a memory is fully remembered, integrated, and emotionally processed, no matter how horrible that memory is, it ceases to be troubling and becomes just another memory in the story of your life. I and countless others are living proof of this truth. I don't understand why we are built that way—Freud's "talking cure" is truly miraculous—but we are. We need to tell our full story, if only to ourselves, in order to heal.

There is something in us—call it the soul, the self, or the deep unconscious—that wants to fully acknowledge everything that ever happened to us. If we have repressed a memory, we will be troubled by the effects of that undigested memory forever, whether we realize it or not. As a yogic practitioner, and someone who does past life regressions, I have observed that traumatic memories can even migrate beyond death and into new lifetimes. To heal fully, the mind needs to locate an event in its time-space point. We need to know what, when, where, and who for a memory to release us. Otherwise, we will be plagued with mental and physical symptoms. Our minds need convincing evidence that "that was then, this is now," and a solid memory is that evidence.

Our fears and phobias are a kind of remembering "through the glass darkly." In the months before my memory came forward, I had become irrationally angry at older men, whom I called "geezers" in my mind every time I saw them. This "memory" was a tightening of the gut, a flushing of the body, and dark thoughts directed at total strangers. Having been in therapy and a therapist myself for so many years, I knew I wasn't crazy or bad. I was curious about these thoughts, but I couldn't access the reality, the knowing of memory until I could. Most people without the touchstone of an integrated memory live with these kinds of symptoms and get a diagnosis: OCD, panic disorder, generalized anxiety disorder, bipolar disorder, and others. Clinicians describe the client as having intrusive thoughts, ideas of reference, compulsions, irritability, and many other symptoms. People read self-help books in the psychology section and end up pathologizing themselves (I've done it too!). They feel their thoughts are irrational and jump down the hole of self-diagnosis or even self-loathing rather than understand that memories lie at the root of many of their symptoms and diagnoses. Clinical understanding taken from books rather than wisdom and experience can push therapists and their clients further away from healing. We have sayings in medicine that reflect that reality, such as "The doctor who treats themselves has a fool for a patient" or "A little knowledge is a terrible thing."

Cognitive Behavioral Therapy

The common feeling of failure due to continued suffering post-treatment explains why so many of us have a viscerally negative reaction to cognitive behavioral therapy (CBT). The name says it all. CBT doesn't treat suffering, nor was it designed to. "Behavioral therapy." CBT treats behavior through cognition; it does not resolve traumas or help surface memories. CBT works with everything in the human mind except repressed or nonverbal memory. One can decrease symptoms and increase functionality (capitalistic productivity) with CBT, but one cannot ever fully heal. "Oh, but it's evidence based," the insurance companies cry. Yes, if your evidence does not include a comprehensive look at human suffering. And it doesn't. Research in my field looks at behavior and diagnosis over a short period of time (three to six months), rarely the subjective experience of suffering over a long period of time. As a result, I, and other colleagues who are trauma experts, end up with what I call CBT refugees. These people, mostly women, are still suffering despite years of trying to manage their thoughts and bodily reactions, and they feel like failures because they feel they have done CBT wrong, compounding their original traumas with feelings of despair and low self-esteem. CBT is not a theoretical base of treatment; it is a set of tools. Some of those tools can be helpful for a phase of clinical work, but they are only helpful in the short term.

Traumatic memories, like zombies, never stay buried. You can try to shovel them into a deeper, more fortified hole, but truth will out. There is a branch of CBT that attempts to work with memories, but only ones that are already fully excavated. Prolonged exposure, where the client is strongly encouraged to walk back into painful memories and situations, is forceful and often does not leave the pace to the sufferer. This approach is exactly the opposite of the memory approach used by seasoned clinicians who realize that people with trauma histories are allergic to force of any kind and can be greatly destabilized even by a single ill-placed question or remark. Experienced and well-trained therapists understand that timing is everything. When it is time for the memories to come, when the client is safe, stabilized, and developmentally ready, they will spontaneously rise up into consciousness, like whales taking a breath.

I am happy if you or someone you know has been helped by CBT. Some clients can work with many kinds of approaches with a lot of resilience. In my practice, I've known more people who have been more harmed than helped by CBT as a sole treatment modality, including treaters themselves. In one workshop I gave, a frustrated clinician raised their hand and asked what to do when they had run through all the CBT worksheets with a client. They had been working together for over a year and they had run out of ideas for treatment. Cue forehead slap. Go back to relational therapy, I answered, and learn about psychodynamics. CBT is a superficial approach, literally and figuratively. It works with thoughts in the cortex. When it doesn't work, the answer is to go deeper into the psyche and the brain. Not all therapists know how to do this kind of depth work, which requires rigorous training, supervision, and self-knowledge.

After more than forty-five years in the field, I can say with certainty that our entire mental health system (if not the entire healthcare system) is based on diagnosis and treatment of what are mostly symptoms and bodily reactions caused by stress and trauma of one sort or another. How our body (including the brain) handles stress and trauma seems largely influenced by genetics and resources. Two people can suffer the same event (and often do, as siblings). One sibling might cope by developing dissociative disorders (OSDD, DID), and one might become a narcissist who identifies with the perpetrator. Both disorders are solutions to the problem at hand for the child: intolerable pain and terror that threaten the child's ability to want to stay alive. Both conditions can resolve successfully with memory work, although it may be harder for the narcissist to want to do this work because they have had so much secondary gain (pleasurable reward) for not remembering and for maintaining their sense of entitlement.

Integrative Acceptance and Memory Work

So if not CBT, what treatments do work to help heal and verify memory, ending the suffering of trauma forever? Here is my very simple answer, distilled down after reading thousands of pages, talking to dozens of colleagues, attending workshops, and treating patients over four decades:

Any therapy where there is a safe, caring attachment to a boundaried healer who can be fully present and empathic to the reality of the client's memories will result in the full healing and integration of traumatic memory over time.

Yes, I said "healer," not therapist. The category of healer includes but is not limited to therapists. I've observed people recover and integrate memories in yoga therapy, weekend workshops, Indigenous healing ceremonies such as sweat-lodges, past life therapies, Reiki healings, rebirthing, acupuncture, and others. Not everyone has the desire or temperament for therapy. Not everyone is ready for therapy as their first healing modality. Not everyone heals one-on-one. Some people feel safer to recover and process memories in large groups or less Northern European (some might say colonial) modalities.

Since insurance has cracked down on the kinds of long-term treatments that facilitate complete integration and healing of traumatic memories, it is very good news that there are other options for people to get help. Don't be fooled by the lack of "evidence." Not every healing modality has organizations that can pay for trauma research. *Lack of research does not equal lack of effectiveness.*

That being said, therapy with a trauma expert can be one of the quickest roads to healing. Many of us already use some or many of the modalities I've mentioned. Meeting with a caring psychotherapist weekly, over the time it takes to heal, ensures safety and stability, as long as the therapist is knowledgeable and has done the personal work it takes to sit with someone with a great deal of trauma.

Here are some of the qualities you will want to look for in your trauma therapist:

- Some verification of their expertise, either in long-term supervision or a lengthy training in an internship or fellowship program treating complex trauma
- Belonging to one or more professional organizations specifically focused on healing PTSD and trauma-related disorders and attending their trainings (ISSTD, ISTSS, ATSS, etc.)
- An awareness of the cruel realities of human behavior, and the ability to listen to horrendous stories without dissociating or minimizing (if a

therapist accuses you of being dramatic or making things up, run!)

- Openness to questions, nonjudgmental, and willing to follow your lead
- Knowing theories but placing more emphasis on your experience and reality than said theories—especially important if you have a dissociative system
- A willingness to learn about areas of less competence or awareness (e.g., anti-racism, ritual abuse, dissociation, government secret programs, white supremacy, etc.)

Threshold Work and Denial

When I train therapists, I talk a lot about "threshold work." We all have thresholds of tolerance based on our culture, our upbringing, and our exposure to negative realities. The three thresholds that therapists and clients encounter in believing histories are horror, spiritual, and reality. Once a threshold is crossed, we enter into denial or unbelief. When a therapist fails to believe a client's story, the result can be catastrophic to the patient and to the therapy.

One of the major obstacles to clients believing their own stories is that they had to suppress the reality of those stories to survive their childhood. Most children are quite good at this, since imaginative play is an essential way for kids to process reality. I'll give you a fairly benign example. My sister and I, aged four and five years, respectively, were often left unsupervised at play time due to my mother's pregnancy, the result being many fights and tears that led to punishment. One day, one of us (I can no longer remember who) came up with a bright idea, "Oh, I know. Let's play that we are sisters who get along! I'll call you Sis, and you call me Sis!" This creative, if somewhat dissociative, solution actually worked well for a time and avoided fights that got us in trouble.

In extreme trauma, the imaginative solution is usually a variation on "That never happened to me" or, occasionally, "That happened to someone else." One client who had some awareness in a moment as a teenager caught himself saying, "I can forget about this when it's over; I can forget about it later," over and over to himself in the midst of a traumatic scenario. The memory of his active employment of denial and forgetting led to him being able to remember earlier traumas as the treatment went on, because he now had the touchstone of "remembering to forget."

Trauma survivors place so much psychic energy into various means of denial and forgetting that when the therapist jumps on the ambivalence bandwagon as well and asks, "What is the evidence that this happened to you?" it immediately increases the level of internal conflict the person experiences between remembering and forgetting. Skepticism increases anxiety and can rupture the therapeutic attachment. Trauma survivors need a lot of support to remember. No one wants to think that people they loved with all their heart hurt them on purpose; yet so often the case is that the person was injured by people who were supposed to love and care for them.

Trauma survivors can become obsessed with evidence where there often is none. They may swirl around in their heads for years asking themselves if this traumatic event could have really happened, bouncing back and forth between being sure that nothing like that could have happened and being sure that it did, whatever "it" was, especially if the abuse was bizarre or crossed a believability threshold. This confusion becomes exhausting and dissonant, resulting in the periodic repression and then resurfacing of these questions. They don't realize that asking themselves that question over and over *is* the evidence. People whose childhood was genuinely safe and loving do not obsess about questions of potential hidden abuse.

Evidence and Remembering

Did that really happen to me? The first response to that question, for most people, is to look for evidence. Clients will comb through medical records, court records, family histories, and photo albums. Only in the rarest cases do findable records even exist. In my own practice, I estimate that less than 10 percent of my clients have access to any definitive records that their abuse even happened. Even rarer is the patient who has obvious scarring from their trauma. Out of dozens of clients, only two have shown up with definitive court and mental health evidence for their extensive abuse history. They had no physical scarring at all. Out of those dozens of clients, only one has shown up with definitive scarring that indicated abuse. They had no record of child abuse being reported at all because their abuse, like so many, occurred in the context of organized crime (i.e., trafficking). My clients who were tortured and abused in secret government programs, of course, have no records at all and usually very few memories when they first arrive in treatment, just as their handlers intended.

In such an evidence-based culture, it is hard for people to wrap their heads around how child abuse can be so prevalent, yet the "evidence" be so scanty. Let's talk about this. I have the unique perspective of having worked in both child protective services and as a long-term psychotherapist for child abuse survivors. Very few of us have worked on both sides of that equation. What has surprised me over the years is how much of a gap exists between the stories I heard on the hotline versus the stories I have heard in my private practice.

I worked at the Judge Baker Children's Center Child-at-Risk Hotline for four years while putting myself through graduate school. We covered the state of Massachusetts after-hours for child abuse and neglect, 4 p.m. to 8 a.m. Sunday to Thursday, and all day on the weekends. I was one of four or five supervisors who oversaw making decisions about calls across the entire state. We screened decisions on mandated and nonmandated child protection reports called into the hotline, and supervised telephone case screeners who took calls regarding abuse and neglect of children in state custody. As supervisors, we initiated emergency responses as needed with both the police and with on-call supervisors for the Department of Social Services, who could dispatch social workers to any location at any hour. On any given night in the early 1990s, there were five to eight screeners reporting to one supervisor, answering dozens of calls, and filing five to twenty reports for child abuse screening and response. Every single report had to be "run by" myself or another supervisor. Over four years, I estimate that I heard over 10,000 stories of child abuse reported by both professionals (police, teachers, doctors, social workers, etc.) and citizens.

Areas of overlap between hotline and private practice seem obvious: reports of physical and sexual abuse, especially where there were obvious physical findings: bruises, abrasions, slap marks, or more serious injuries (e.g., broken bones). There were more types of hotline reports that I did not hear about as a therapist: burns, falls, environmental neglect, medical neglect, food deprivation, and medical treatment for early abuse (infancy to about age eight years).

A surprisingly common report on the hotline was a medical report of inflicted burns, especially immersion, or "sock," burns, where a child's feet are held in scalding water. These were always reported by a medical professional, often at Boston

Children's Hospital (across the street from the hotline). According to the Department of Justice Report *Burn Injuries in Child Abuse* (2001), 10 percent of all child abuse cases are burn cases—fairly common. Yet I have never once heard about sock burns from a client, a colleague with trauma clients, or people I supervise with trauma cases. I've never read a research paper on the traumatic results of early childhood burn injuries in any psychology journal, although I did find an article in the *Annals of Burns and Fire Disasters* (Lodha, Karia, and DeSousa 2020) talking about PTSD in their young patients. Why? Here is a potential clue: According to this same report, "child abuse burn victims are almost always under the age of ten years with the majority under the age of two years." The young age of the victim leaves plenty of time for healing, and these kinds of burns often heal without scarring to wonder about. Even with scarring, the child is still left with only the parent's explanation, which will typically not include any admission of guilt. The parent may not talk about nor even remember the incident themselves due to their dissociation or denial.

The younger the child is, the less likely they are to have narrative memory—the memory that tells the story of what happened. They may have somatic (body) memory, perhaps manifesting in an intense dislike of tubs and hot pools, but they will not know from whence this aversion arises. In fact, any early abuse that ranges from infancy to about eight years of age may be easily forgotten because of the plasticity of the brain, a topic we will return to. Children who are abused at those early ages, even if they are medically or legally documented, may not have access to those records or to an adult who wants to (or is able to) tell them about their early childhood traumas. These children grow into adults unaware that they were victims of serious violence and trauma in their youth.

On the therapist side, I have heard many abuse histories for which there was no medical treatment, no family oral history, no acknowledgment that these events had happened in reality to the child at all. For instance, I've heard a surprising number of stories about small children being confined and abandoned for hours at a time in a tiny box indoors or even out in the woods. At first, these clients had no idea why they had these memories or why this was done to them. It turned out that all these clients had been sex-trafficked as children. After a lot of work with each of them, we discovered the same reason for the confinement. Abandoned confinement was early training for shipping these children for the sex trade. As one of my clients put it, "Sex-trafficked children smell like gasoline and urine." Urine because they were kept in boxes past their ability to hold their bladder, and gasoline because they were confined on boats, the back of Humvees, and other vehicles. None of these clients lived in the same state, and they did not know each other. Was there ever a report on the Child-At-Risk Hotline of children being shipped in boxes? No. Never. The traffickers plan with cunning and savvy. They almost certainly paid off, with cash or privileges, people who might have discovered these kids along the way. They had their own network of doctors who treated injured kids, and those docs were not calling in abuse reports. The way they conducted operations ensured safety for themselves and their precious cargo. Child sex trafficking was and continues to be a multi-billion-dollar business.

Abuser groups, by definition, keep no evidence. They destroy evidence. Families that abuse their children deny and suppress information to their children lest their kids report them to the authorities or sue them one day. Children are absolutely at the mercy of adults. If adults don't want them to know about their own history, they won't! If a child starts to remember or confront abuse the parent will say, "That never happened!" or worse.

The odds are heavily stacked against adults remembering their abuse as kids. When adults start to remember, society screams "false memory" because the public was hoodwinked into thinking that therapists somehow have an agenda to "implant memories." I study mind control and help people heal from it. Memory implantation is possible, but it is arduous work requiring expertise in hypnosis and often torture. Aside from the fact that the vast majority of therapists went into this profession to help people, not hurt them, there is also the reality that we are just not paid enough to put effort into creating implanted memories, even if we knew how and wanted to. If we did, somehow, want to do mind control, wouldn't we implant happy memories instead of horrifying ones, in order to cover our tracks? The whole "implanted memory" narrative makes no sense at all. The only people who fool around with memories are those with ill intent who seek to create plausible deniability for their own heinous criminal actions.

When a client, loaded up with dissociation, denial, or programming, does finally begin to remember their trauma against all odds, the therapist's job is to join with them and help point them in the direction of meaningful evidence. The primary evidence is the client's own narrative, their own true story, and the combining of all the memory puzzle pieces to create a whole, believable memory. Once the client is whole enough to believe themselves and has enough ego strength to act, they can then pursue other types of evidence, evidence that might even hold up in a court of law. This healing process can take many years. Sadly, by the time a client is ready to press charges after arduous therapy work, the statute of limitations has often already run out for criminal charges.

Memory Components

I want to preface this section by saying that there is an appropriate season to remembering that naturally occurs from around forty years old onward. If memories come upon clients too early in their life, their adulting skills may collapse and they could even have a psychotic break. If too late, they are too physically feeble to handle the effects of those memories in their system. I had a friend whose father started remembering his childhood sexual abuse in his nineties as his memory compartments started collapsing. He did not have the physical strength at that point in his life to heal successfully, and he suffered tremendously.

The body/mind has its own organic timing for processing—or as Chinese medicine would say, digesting—traumatic events. Often the earliest traumatic events are processed the latest in life. Good trauma therapy provides a safe place and pace for remembering. Forcing memories is never the answer and can create more problems than are solved. The body/mind, what I like to call the 200,000-year-old computer, knows when it is the right time to remember and re-integrate.

Under extreme stress, if one is young, the brain has an effective divide-and-conquer strategy for making memories manageable. The brain cannot get rid of a memory, but it can divide the memory into components and store them in different neurological compartments. You can think of this like separating oxygen and fire. Stored apart, no problem. If they come together, an explosion happens. This analogy is not an exaggeration. A newly integrated memory can shatter life as a person once knew it, their sense of identity, their history, and their family. It can also render a person unfunctional for a time and, in rare cases, cause a person to complete suicide.

So, what are these components that make up a complete

memory? Take a moment and see for yourself. Go inward for a few minutes and think of a really happy memory, a lovely untriggering time of your life. Pick one and really inhabit that memory. Got it? Okay, now what are the elements of that memory? How do you know that it is a real memory and not a fantasy? Spend a few moments and really identify all the elements that create that true memory. Good.

If you wish, you can even jot them down in writing; as you write out the different components that make up the memory, you may see patterns.

Usually when I ask people to do this exercise, three main components emerge. The first is the narrative—what is happening. The narrative is the story: there is a beginning, middle, and ending. There exists a pre- and post-narrative, what happened before and after that moment in time.

Let's say your memory is walking down the aisle of your wedding. The narrative might be *I am walking down the aisle of the church toward my spouse, the wedding party, and the pastor because I'm about to be married.* You know that earlier in the day you were getting ready and earlier than that there was a story to your relationship. You know that afterward you went to your hotel or left for your honeymoon, and you know that you entered into married life. That is narrative, the verbal story of what happened.

Another component of that memory is how you felt. Maybe you felt more than one thing. You may have felt deliriously happy, peacefully content, grateful, in love, or other positive emotions. There may also have been some negative emotions. Maybe someone in the wedding party was annoying you that day, or you had anxiety about everything going as planned. Maybe you were hungry or overstimulated. So this component is about your internal state of being, your inner feelings or, as we say clinically, your interoception (inner perception), that informs you about your emotions.

The third category of memory is sensory input—what you are seeing, hearing, smelling, touching, and tasting during the event. Maybe you remember seeing the smile on your spouse's face, the smell of flowers, the sound of the processional being played, the feeling on your finger of your ring being placed by your spouse. Later you may remember the taste of your wedding cake or sumptuous treats ordered for the reception.

The narrative, the inner feelings, and the sensory inputs create a memory. These components locate the memory in time, space, and context, making the event feel real and evidential. Without all three components integrated, a memory does not feel real. It feels like a fantasy or even like a random, if persistent, thought or feeling. When we read a book, we only have narrative; we know that we are not in the book. When we watch a movie, we only have narrative and the sensory input that the movie hands us. We know because of how we feel that we are not actually inside that movie. Only when narrative, sensory input, and internal feeling states join do we know, without a doubt, that we are in an actual personal memory.

Most people I have worked with have at least one persistent memory fragment. It could be a "snapshot" picture in their mind that confuses them with its persistence. In my book *Wisdom, Attachment, and Love in Trauma Therapy* (Pease Banitt 2018), I discuss a client who said they felt like they must be a "bad person" because they had such bad pictures in their head. It turned out that those pictures were related to actual events, and the client was only able to realize this when they started to cry thinking about the mental image, something they had never done before. The spontaneous feeling of extreme sorrow integrating with the snapshot helped them start accepting their reality. After processing this integration, the narrative emerged to create a complete memory.

Persistent unexplained somatic states can also be memory fragments. These states can be back or pelvic pain, headaches, depression, anxiety, and even chronic conditions like asthma or sore throats. After the client fully goes through the pain of remembering and abreacting (discharging the emotions), these physical and psychiatric issues simply melt away. I'm not saying this work is easy, but it is effective in relieving suffering.

Occasionally people have a persistent narrative fragment without any sensory input. A very common one is the fragment I started this chapter with, "I think I was molested," or, in my practice, "I think I might have been subjected to ritual abuse." Sometimes the narrative fragment includes the identity of the perpetrator(s); often it does not. When a person (or a therapist) fills in the blanks with a guess, it is not helpful legally or inter-personally. A good therapist will help the sufferer be patient in sitting with uncertainty until more information comes to light. Narrative fragments are common but are some of the easiest to deny because they do not cause physical or emotional suffering unlike the emotional and sensory fragments. If a therapist is a keen observer, a narrative fragment may be easy to spot because the body will sometimes reveal itself with dramatic flushing or blotchiness unnoticed by the client.

The Myth of Objective Memory

Memory answers the questions who, what, where, when, why, and how you felt about it—your unique subjective experience. Let's be clear. All memories are subjective. There is no such thing as an objective memory. We all stand in our unique point of time, space, and consciousness. No two beings' memories could ever be exactly the same; it is not even a possibility.

Generally, we accept this without fuss. Except when it comes to traumatic memory.

Here's an example. If you ask me what I had for dinner last night and I say roast beef, but later I remember that it really was turkey, and I had roast beef two nights ago, you would not call me a liar for changing my story. You would understand that memory can be faulty and that I just had a memory glitch. If my partner said the turkey was dry and I said it was delicious, you would not accuse me of manipulating your opinion of the turkey; you would assume I had a different experience of the turkey than my partner. No biggie. If later I remembered we also had pumpkin pie, your response would likely be curiosity rather than criticism. "How was it?" Not "You are making things up!" Acceptance of and curiosity about another's reality is a necessary part of social discourse. Yet therapists and other medical professionals are often taught to question the patient's reality as if they may be liars or manipulators rather than people seeking to talk about and understand their traumatic experiences. Naturally people's stories are going to change with time. They always do, whether we are talking about dinner or sexual abuse. And their stories are always going to be different than their abuser's story (way different!) or an observer's story.

Why do we as therapists, and as a society in general, hold traumatic memories to a higher level of evidence and proof than other memories? Why do we assume that the victim is manipulative, attention-getting, drug-seeking, or exaggerating? I have come to believe the answer lies in the very ocean we swim in, patriarchal culture.

Patriarchy and Remembering

The force in society that causes dissociation, and the suppression of memory, is patriarchy itself. Hear me out. Northern

European and American culture still tends to look up to grandiose, larger-than-life narcissistic personalities while denigrating people who are empathic and dissociative—even though narcissists and psychopaths are responsible for most of the ills of the world. For those folks to hang on to power, they have to deny and suppress disclosures of abuses caused by the systems that have supported their rise to power. They have to be abusive strongmen who appear appealing and sympathetic. This is clearly what a large segment of the population still wants as a leader. We, as a people, are very conflicted because we believe that ruthless use of power will protect us, while at the same time needing human love and compassion to rule the day.

Patriarchy demands that we be strong, unempathic ("no softies!"), achievement oriented, not "sensitive snowflakes." But most of all, patriarchy demands that we uphold the rights of men over the rights of women and children; this is the very definition of the word. When women started claiming their rights, their right to vote, their right to name abusers, their right to prosecute their abusers and their children's abusers, they were standing up to the patriarchy and starting to balance the power equation. Women even had to name the movement: #MeToo (Caprino 2018).

In a patriarchal society, there is no language for abuse, because to be abusive, to maintain one's power and pleasure by force, is considered a right of men and in many cases is considered admirable and just. It was not that long ago that we had a "rule of thumb"—the width of a stick allowed for beating your wife into submission. In such a structure, remembering and speaking out is criminalized. Women and men alike collude to keep abusive people in power by their silence. As the ancient maxim goes, "*Qui tacet consentit,*" silence lends consent. *Silence is necessary to uphold patriarchy.* Every totalitarian government seeks to suppress women by every avenue possible and, especially, to silence their voices. When a woman has been fully acculturated to patriarchal society, she will suppress her memory to suppress her own voice, and she will suppress other women's voices, even her daughters'. Memories demand expression. No memory, no inner conflict around expression. You see how this works?

Fortunately, the tide is turning. Women are remembering. Women are talking to each other, talking on social media, and confronting abusers with the truth. #MeToo. This confrontation is *necessary* to healing personal and society's ills. It's not drama, it's trauma!

When we free ourselves from the abusive demands of patriarchy, we will have the option to turn around and help free men if we wish to. Men are also victims of violence and need help to remember, heal, and speak their truths. They also need to be held accountable for their abuses of power. Women with long memories and free voices can hold up a mirror to patriarchy and take the legal actions necessary to ensure a more balanced society. Good men will join them.

The more we speak, the more we will remember. The more we remember, the more we can heal. The more we can heal, the more highly we can function. The more highly we can function, the more healthy, beneficial, balanced, and peaceful our society will become, and the happier we will be as proud people, free to be loving, secure, and powerful.

References

Caprino, Kathy. "Renowned Therapist Explains the Crushing Effects of Patriarchy on Men and Women Today." *Forbes*, January 26, 2018. Accessed December 26, 2022. www.forbes.com/sites/kathycaprino/2018/01/25/renowned-therapist-explains-the-crushing-effects-of-patriarchy-on-men-and-women-today/.

Herman, Judith L. *Trauma and Recovery: The Aftermath of Violence – From Domestic Abuse to Political Terror*. New York: Basic Books, 2022.

Lodha, P., B. Shah, S. Karia, and A. De Sousa. "Post-Traumatic Stress Disorder (PTSD) Following Burn Injuries: A Comprehensive Clinical Review." *Annals of Burns and Fire Disasters* 33, no. 4 (2020): 276–87.

Pease Banitt, S. *The Trauma Tool Kit: Healing PTSD from the Inside Out*. Wheaton, IL: Quest Books, 2012.

Pease Banitt, S. *Wisdom, Attachment, and Love in Trauma Therapy: Beyond Evidence-Based Practice*. New York: Routledge, 2018.

US Department of Justice, Office of Justice Programs. *Burn Injuries in Child Abuse*. June 2001. Accessed February 8, 2023. https://www.ojp.gov/pdffiles/91190-6.pdf.

Chapter 2

Addiction as Dissociation

A Survivor's Tale

Jamie Marich, PhD,
LPCC-S, REAT, RYT-500

My fascination with the brown, magical powder began innocently enough. During my elementary school years, one of the most connecting experiences I enjoyed with my increasingly withdrawing mother was helping her bake.

"Here, Jamie, lick the spoon," or "Do you want to lick the bowl?" she'd offer.

Yes, the cake mix batter, cool and gooey and ready to go into the oven, was amazing. One day when she wasn't looking, as we got everything set on the kitchen counter, I wondered how the powder itself would taste. It always looked so yummy, and my five-year-old curiosity got the best of me. I began sticking my finger in the bowl, scooping what little powder I could before secretly licking it off my finger. One time when she stepped away, I worked my way up to taking in an entire teaspoon. The first time I swallowed a spoonful of Duncan Hines chocolate cake mix, I found heaven right here on earth.

My imagination and internal world already very active in coping with the mounting dysfunction in our home. My father's conversion to a radical version of evangelical Christianity made everything worse. I retreated into my bedroom every evening to play with my dolls and dive further into these creative landscapes that protected me from reality. That cake mix became one more thing that helped me easily find some semblance of escapist pleasure. After that spoonful moment in the kitchen, I worked up the courage to start sneaking boxes from my mother's pantry and hiding them in my room. Ever the power shopper, she bought them ten for a dollar. I was careful enough to not be noticed and rationed myself to just one table-spoon a day through most of elementary school. Even when I ended up losing a great deal of weight at a rapid pace to pursue sports more fully in the eighth grade, I never denied myself the cake mix.

Although cake mix was my favorite secret treat, likely due to the simultaneous flour and sugar rush it provided, other foods would also comfort me, especially at the dinner table where my mom and dad would often fight. Looking back on it now, it felt like I dissociated into the delicious meals in order to drown them out. Some professionals would say that I exhibited signs of disordered eating or that food was my first addiction. My first, yes, because I would go on to develop others—to alcohol, to drugs, to work, and to the warm embrace of performance recognition. Others might hesitate to use the word *addiction*, feeling it is too stigmatizing and representative of an antiquated disease model. They would describe my deep dives into the Duncan Hines as a trauma response, and my overindulgence in other, seemingly more dangerous things later in my life as the evidence of untreated trauma. As an addiction specialist and an addiction survivor, I firmly believe the answer is a both/and.

Yes, I developed addictions.

And those addictions were the natural progressions of a brain that learned to dissociate early and often.

I've spent the last several years of my professional life

explaining the concept that I now call "addiction as dissocia-tion," a model I developed with a student, friend, and fellow trauma survivor in long-term recovery, Dr. Adam O'Brien. During one of our early collaborative sessions that led to us writing an article for addiction professionals in 2018, we shared our stories of recovery through the traditional disease model and acknowledged the role that 12-step programs played in our early recovery. Yet we both knew that something was lacking. Adam clearly recalls sitting in his first rehab center, hearing the counselor lecture about the disease of addiction, and knowing inside, "There has to be more to this." And although we'd both talked about the role that dissociation played in our lives as part of our consultations, the more we shared with each other, it seemed that our addictions, too, could be framed as advanced progressions of young brains that learned how to dissociate often in order to survive (Marich and O'Brien, 2018).

Of course, as a young child flailing in the waters of spiritual abuse, misogyny, sexual trauma, and school bullying, I didn't know what the word *dissociation* meant. Knowing what I know now as a professional, and as someone who has engaged in loads of my own therapy with trauma and dissociation-compe-tent therapists, dissociating as a child is the reason that I am still here. Two comments that I constantly heard from my parents were, "Jamie looks like she's been beaned in the head with a fastball again" (Dad), and "Jamie was probably off in her own little world when she tripped and fell" (Mom). I/we didn't have the vocabulary to describe what was going on at the time as parts of us became more differentiated. When we endured the worst of our traumatic experiences, it was like we lost a part of ourselves, and several more parts or fragments could break off of those lost children who still lived within and craved real nourishment.

Here is what I know to be true about dissociation after years of studying it, working with others who struggle with dissociative tendencies, and learning my own patterns. Having this base understanding is critical to further understand addiction as dissociation. Dissociation derives from a Latin root word meaning to sever/separate or to divide. Although not a new word, in the 1880s French psychiatrist Pierre Janet began using *dissociation* to refer to the psychological phenomenon he commonly saw accompany trauma. Human beings can separate or divide from the present moment when the present moment becomes unpleasant, painful, stressful, or even boring. All human beings, at one time or another in their lives, have experienced some level of severing from the present moment, even if it's through behaviors like daydreaming, zoning out, feeling floaty, or losing track of time. People with clinically significant dissociative disorders, or those who experience significant dissociation as part of other psychological issues, may dissociate more intensely, yet the phenomenon is inherent to the human experience.

Dissociation can also involve parts or aspects of self being disaggregated from each other, a word that is actually closer to Janet's original term for the phenomenon, *désagrégation*, before it got translated into English by William James as *dissociation*. All human beings are composed of many parts and aspects of self, and, like with dissociation itself, the phenomenon itself is not an instant source for alarm. But when there is disharmony among a person's inner world of parts, especially when that inner world is more differentiated like we see in dissociative disorders, the person may have problems in daily living and functioning. While theories vary on how different parts (sometimes called alters in dissociative disorders) can develop, we can generally assume that healthy attachment is needed for the human brain to develop in a cohesive way.

Several different neurological functions are responsible for the activities of dissociation in all areas of the brain, including the most primitive brainstem that can allow us to shut down, collapse, or freeze to submission in the face of threat. The endogenous opioid system, part of the limbic system, is also involved in dissociative responses. This system causes our brain to release dopamine and create our own natural feel-good chemicals to fight pain. Vital to the addiction as dissociation model is the concept that using certain substances or engaging in some pleasurable behaviors taps into the endogenous opioid system by enhancing the same dopaminergic response. Because this phenomenon can boost natural dopaminergic responses above their baseline or make accessing such responses more immediate, once we learn the power of these chemicals— whether they be cake mix, cocaine, or potentially self-destructive behaviors—we can escape from the present moment more quickly and more intensely.

Some people describe dissociation as the opposite of mindfulness, a comparison that is salient when we consider my favorite definition for mindfulness—the practice of returning to awareness. Although many definitions of mindfulness abound, both religious and secular, the definition I just offered most resonates, and is based on the Sanskrit word *smrti* (the memory of having been aware). If mindfulness is about returning to the present moment and dissociation is fleeing from it, they certainly can appear as opposites. While some of us with dissociative identities do maintain that parts of us can be mindful and other parts of us dissociated at the same time, there seems to be general consensus that learning to practice mindfulness can be difficult for the brain that is so used to dissociating.

And we, as human beings, dissociate for two primary reasons. We dissociate to protect the self or our system of self and parts. Or we dissociate to get our needs met. For those of us who grew up with trauma and developmental wounds as our norm, these reasons generally exist in combination. By the time I left my parents' house at the age of eighteen, even though I'd never heard the word *dissociating* once in my life, I was already an expert at it.

The bridge between food and the more dangerous world of alcohol and drugs came in the form of overachieving and the dopamine hit that winning awards and getting straight A's provided. In elementary school, most of my teachers and peers considered me smart, but that came from being that rather odd kid who studied random facts and excelled at creative pursuits, especially writing and theater. My grades were good, but I was not at the top of my class. Somehow I knew that going from the repressive Catholic elementary school to a clean slate at the public high school would be an opportune time to develop a new identity. Knowing that I had the potential for it, I decided the first day I walked through the doors of Chaney High School in Youngstown, Ohio, that I was going to be valedictorian. Being the smart kid would be my identity, that thing that made me special.

While I naturally excelled at my best subjects—English and the social studies—I made myself do well in math and science, often studying obnoxiously long hours at the expense of my physical health. It all felt worth it to see my mother and grandfather's faces when I brought home yet another straight-A report card. My dad was too wrapped up at his cult-like church to even notice or care, yet getting these warm recognitions from doing well in school did what I'd hoped it'd do. It made me feel special, fending off the pain of a father who constantly made me feel not good enough for one reason or another, mostly because, no matter how hard I tried, I couldn't conform to his model of what being a good Christian should be. After many years and much therapy later, it's clear that I never could have made him happy. He worshiped an abusive, misogynist version of Jesus and the church, and here was I, a queer feminist soul, who never stood a chance of being comfortable as my full self in my home of origin.

I also engaged in just about every academic extracurricular activity I could find, excelling at most of them. I qualified to join the National Speech and Debate Association (formerly National Forensic League) national tournament my senior year of high school, competed three times in the National History Day competition, and even got to compete at the International Science and Engineering Fair during my junior year. Winning local or state prizes in writing or social studies–type competitions came easily to me. And even in the science fair world, I became known as "the one who could really speak." Every trophy, every medal, every ribbon, every certificate was a hit of acknowledgment that I deserved to take up space on this earth and, of course, brought me pleasure in the short term.

And yes, I graduated high school co-valedictorian along with three other classmates for whom all this school stuff seemed to come much more easily. Whenever I share my story in the rooms of 12-step recovery, I make sure to mention that I was valedictorian of my high school class. It's not to brag on myself in any way, it's truly to highlight that anyone can be brought down by addiction. In my senior yearbook, my classmates voted me "Class Brain." Had there been a "Most Likely to End Up in AA" category, people would not have thought of me. Plenty of stereotypical stoners, dropouts, or party people would have seemed much more likely. Untreated pain shows up in all kinds of people, and all kinds of people end up discovering the "sense of ease and comfort," as the Big Book of Alcoholics Anonymous calls it, that ingesting pleasurable chemicals provides.

If I'm really being honest, I was about twelve when I

started dabbling in overusing opiate cough syrup and over-the-counter pills in the vein of Benadryl or Dramamine. These kinds of pills wouldn't get me high, but they provided me with just enough pleasant drowsiness to help me not be here. We had a family doctor who liberally prescribed prescription cough medicines with codeine or other opiates whenever any of us got sick, and of course I would finish mine off early while the rest of the family would inevitably leave some of theirs hanging around.

I stayed in my hometown for college after earning a full scholarship and already completing two years of college while still in high school. My scholarship afforded me the chance to live in the dorms, away from my parents' house and into a whole new world of adjustment. I often struggled with bronchitis. Getting sick as a bodily response to pushing myself too hard was nothing new—I'd also developed some major gastrointestinal issues in high school as a result. When our doctor easily kept writing me liquid codeine, I really began to see why people got addicted to drugs. My fear of getting in trouble prevented me from doing anything illegal to get more, yet my continual illnesses and developing savvy for mixing over-the-counter aids for drowsiness accelerated my problem. Once alcohol entered the picture, I didn't stand a chance of surviving college without a major addiction problem.

Even though alcohol was an important part of celebrations in the Croatian American culture when I was born, my father's conversion to evangelical Christianity when I was five years old cast an immediate shadow over alcohol and all who consumed it in our home. My father believed that drinking alcohol was a sin worthy of hell. Some of the biggest fights that he got into with my mom was over her continued engagement with alcohol and Croatian social settings. Although it's hard for me to admit, getting into trouble with my dad was probably a major factor in why I didn't try much drinking in high school. Yes, I started dabbling with cigarettes around age fifteen and was a full-blown smoker by the time I lived in the dorms. Yet drinking heavily was a line I felt I couldn't cross until I left their house.

My first year in the dorm was mild in comparison to what would then transpire over the next two years. I spent the summer of 1998 studying Croatian language in Zagreb, where the drinking age was only eighteen, and I was an ocean away from my father's judgment. Yes, I fell in love with my ancestral homeland, and I also fell in love with alcohol. Not only did I love the feeling that getting drunk gave me, but it also really did kill the pain of being a social outcast. Although I tried to engage with my peers that summer, people from all over the world who were studying language with me, I still felt like that little kid who would inevitably be bullied by the kids who were much cooler. I had crushes on about three guys in the program that summer. One downright rejected me and the two others were hard to read. Yet getting drunk was predictable. It would consistently make me feel better.

When I returned to Youngstown for the fall quarter, I continued my explorations with chemicals, this time joined by one of my roommates who was also an evangelical girl breaking out of her shell. It seemed like everyone was drinking in college, but it took me a while to notice that people would really steer clear of me the next day when they saw me. I don't remember it all, yet I do know that we did a lot to embarrass ourselves. My second year in the dorms, when I was nineteen going on twenty, I continued to struggle with bronchial illnesses and also experienced the worst traumatic loss in my life up until that point. Mrs. Leone, my beloved high school guidance counselor was my first mentor and a meaningful attachment figure. She died unexpectedly at the age of forty-eight from pneumonia. Her death itself would have been enough to rock my world, but also it ultimately provided the motivation I needed to sever any ties with my father's church. I had become more active in the church during my senior year of high school and I even joined, mostly to keep my father happy. When I told him I didn't want to be a part of his congregation anymore, he tore into me in a way that my brother and I would go on to describe as *mauling*.

He hurled every insult possible at me that night—about my weight, the lost state of my soul, and how no one really thought I was special and no one cared about me. He proclaimed that God took Mrs. Leone from my life as a punishment, as a sign that I'd better "watch out" or God would keep removing people from my life until I turned my life back to Jesus. He said that my mother and brother would be next. With that line, my brother, who was thirteen at the time and overhearing all of this, came to my defense and demanded that my father back down. (As my brother grew older, he became less and less afraid of my father, and he not only took him on, he would go on to be a great comfort to me as well—at an age when children should not have to be taking care of siblings. I often say that my brother and I survived the Titanic of our parents' marriage together and, in many ways, parented each other.)

I was catatonic in the corner of the living room before my brother put me and my tears to bed. The entire experience of Mrs. Leone's death, and the abuse from my father that followed, caused one of my dissociative parts to form. I don't really remember how I got out of the house the next day, what happened in the weeks that followed, or how and when I even spoke to my father again. Life went on in a fog, and there would be a lot of amnesia until I would go back to Croatia in September 1999 for my cousin's wedding. That interlude seemed to bring me back to life for a bit. During that trip was when I first had the inspiration to move there for a year to teach English while I figured out what on earth I wanted to do with my life. Because for the first time ever, my grades were starting to suffer. I still graduated from college summa cum laude. I graduated summa cum laude, with the highest possible honors, yet still felt aimless.

I went through the motions of starting a graduate program in history so that I could stay close to a boy I fell in love with. In the fall of 2000, it became clear that while the boy liked hanging out with me, he did not have the same level of feelings for me, which took my alcohol and pill use to darker places. While I did not actively research how much of each it would have taken to end my life, I regularly binged on these chemical mixtures and truly didn't care if I ever woke up.

After a particularly bad binge on Thanksgiving weekend 2000, I knew it was time to finally make my way to Europe. Although some people in recovery would have judged what I did as a geographical cure—hoping that the change of scenery would be enough to fix me—I am glad that I followed whatever moment of clarity fluttered in my heart that told me to go. Because during the two and a half years I ended up spending in the Croatian enclave of Bosnia-Herzegovina (2000–03), I met the people who I needed to meet in order to heal.

The full story of this amazing adventure appears in my memoir *You Lied to Me about God . . . and Other Tales of Spiritual Abuse Recovery.* For discussing addiction as dissociation, I'll relay the highlights here. I ended up working in Medjugorje, Bosnia-Herzegovina, for the Catholic parish of St. James and their various pilgrim outreach and social programs. Medjugorje is the site of an alleged apparition of the Blessed Virgin Mary to six village children in 1981, and many people in Medjugorje continue to experience apparitions of her in some form to this day. It's one of the most popular sites for pilgrimage in the modern Catholic world, attracting both the faithful and the curious from all around the world. One person in particular would carry me the message of recovery in a trauma and dissociation-informed manner.

Her name was Janet Leff, an American social worker and devout Catholic who was in long-term recovery from alcoholism. Janet had made twelve previous pilgrimages to Medjugorje, including many aid-related missions during the war that raged through the countries that formerly composed Yugoslavia from 1991 to 1995. In her retirement, she decided to stay in Medjugorje long-term and assist with some early treatment and community initiatives that were starting to follow the war. As a longtime member of Alcoholics Anonymous, she facilitated several meetings a week in the church basement of St. James's rectory for pilgrims, as well as any locals who wanted to attend.

I liked Janet upon meeting her, and our first source of connection was both being from Ohio. Janet had no Slavic ancestry and spoke almost none of the language, so she primarily worked with hired interpreters when going to local events. That July, she would be attending a county-level meeting on alcoholism and addiction, in Croatian. None of her interpreters were available, so she asked me to come and do my best to help her understand the proceedings.

On the drive back to the small village of Medjugorje, I asked her many questions, wondering if many of the patterns in my own dysfunctional family were related to alcoholism. She gave me a translated text of the Alcoholics Anonymous Big Book in Croatian, saying, "Here, you may find this interesting. And it may help you with the language." Janet knew that I would benefit from a recovery program. Yet she didn't try to force it on me. She was simply open to conversation and connection. About a month later, when I used pills again—pills that I stole—I knew I could confide in her.

"I don't understand, Janet," I said, "I've been clean for the eight months I've lived here. I've been doing the church thing and feeling better. Why did I use?"

She helped me understand that even though I hadn't taken pills or other drugs during that time, I was still drinking. She famously said to me, "To tweak that famous song a bit, when you're not near the drug you love, you'll love the drug you're with."

That was me!

We talked for three hours that day, as I shared most of my life story with her. And she responded after hearing me out with, "Jamie, the good news is I think you're an alcoholic, an addict, or both."

"How is that good news?" I replied.

"It's good news because we know what to do about it," she said, going on to explain the disease model of addiction in which she believed. That felt like dangerous ground at first, recalling the things my father believed about calling addiction a disease being the work of Satan and the scientific secular world. Yet as Janet spoke, I knew I was hearing the truth. I had an illness that needed to be treated. And while it took me a year of these hard conversations with Janet and going to meetings to finally accept that I needed to be proactive in treating my illness, this relationship formed the basis of my recovery that still sustains me today.

"Jamie, after everything you've been through, it's no wonder you turned out to be addicted. What are you going to do about it now?" She affirmed and then challenged. This guidance she gave me that day is still the foundational motivation of my recovery and heartily informs how I've gone on to work with others.

When I released the first edition of my book *Trauma and the 12 Steps* in 2012, a podcaster asked me what I hoped the book would accomplish. Both editions (the revised and expanded version published in 2020) brought in my professional insights on how we can update the 12 steps and related principles for the times, considering all that we've learned about trauma since the fellowship of Alcoholics Anonymous was founded in 1935. Yet my simplified answer to the podcaster came like a flash: "I want everyone seeking recovery, especially 12-step recovery, to have an experience like I had with Janet. Because she was trauma-informed before I realized what that even meant."

Another turning-point moment in my recovery journey with Janet came a few months after our first conversation about the disease of addiction and why she believed I had it. My boss, a kind yet very traditional Franciscan priest, asked me to take some American pilgrims on a tour of the children's home where I taught and tutored English. Of course, I had to say yes because it was work, yet this last-minute obligation forced me to cancel my music lesson with another visiting priest. These lessons had become a very nourishing and healing time for me, and rescheduling with that priest was not always easy due to his schedule. My boss did nothing wrong, yet I completely melted down on him, and he just didn't know what to do. He ended up calling Janet, who showed up at the parish rectory to scrape me quite literally off the floor and get me back to my apartment.

I do remember hearing her say to him, "Father, this isn't a little girl overreacting, this is a post-traumatic reaction."

It was the first time anyone had used the word *trauma* to refer to my experience.

Ever the gifted healer, Janet got me into my apartment and, like my brother did on that night of the mauling, guided me to bed to lie down. She brought me a glass of water and placed a cold compress on my head as my tears gradually started to subside. Then she gently guided me into a conversation that was free of shame or judgment. And she was able to explain to me what she meant by a post-traumatic reaction.

"But, Janet," I said, "I never went to war. I never even survived a war like the people that we work with here."

"Maybe," she replied, "the war zone was your house. And Skid Row was your bedroom. Trauma takes on all different kinds of forms, Jamie."

Janet not only sponsored my recovery, she sponsored my transformation. She also guided me in some introspection around the role that dissociation played in my life. She helped me understand that the world of daydream and fantasy I escaped into as a child kept me alive. Yet at a certain point as I was confronted with navigating the realities of adult life, this coping skill backfired on me. Alcohol and drugs increasingly enabled me to escape reality instead of dealing with it.

The early recovery tools she taught me were helpful, a collection of 12 step standards and some skills that I would later learn to be mindfulness. Janet taught me about working with simple activities of daily living to develop a healthy routine. We also developed a prayer together. Even though religious trauma was a big part of my story, I never really stopped believing in God. I just needed a 12-step sponsor with a gentle touch to teach me the idea of *God as I understand God*, and in meetings I realized that I was dealing with a God who loved me.

"God, show me reality," became a simple and sustaining prayer that got me through early recovery. And even though my spirituality has evolved since my stint in working for the institutional church, embracing a wide variety of wisdom paths, this core prayer still works. Sometimes I augment to, "God/Goddess/Divine Mother, help me to deal with reality."

I was surprised when, not too long into my recovery, Janet recommended I go back to graduate school to study counseling.

This idea initially startled me because I didn't even like psychology as an undergraduate student!

"Jamie, I see how you are with the kids here," she explained. You relate to them. You get them. Pain knows pain. You've learned the art of being a good helper over here. Now you just have to go back to school and learn the technical stuff."

Of course, Janet cautioned, I would probably need to seek out a counselor specifically for some deeper work on trauma and family of origin issues when I returned to the United States to start my graduate program in the fall of 2003. I attended some general cognitive-behavioral sessions with a campus counselor for that first year, but working my first full semester of clinical internship in the summer showed me that I needed something more.

I interned at a typical medical-model residential treatment facility for children and adolescents. Even though I had a supervisor who supported my interests using the expressive arts in therapy, something about the overall vibe of the hospital simply revolted me. It wasn't the children who triggered me. It was the doctors, staff, case workers, and juvenile justice representatives whom I observed participating in and upholding a toxic system that felt unpleasantly familiar. Couple all of that with another heartbreak in my personal life, and it was really hard to stay present at work.

A few staff members started to ask things like, "Are you here with us? Because you look really far off."

A young therapist I befriended at the facility ended up conducting the needed intervention. Because of our good relationship, he knew he could go there.

"Jamie," he said, "you are dissociating all of the time. And unless you get more of the right kind of therapy to address it, you are not going to last in this field."

He was right. I'd had two years of continuous sobriety. And

although I highly regarded my recovery and didn't want to lose it, on most days I still struggled with suicidal thoughts and impulses to self-injure.

What happened to me was a clear case of the primary addiction (i.e., drugs and alcohol) clearing up, and the trauma-based dissociation that formed its foundation still being there. Twelve-step traditionalists will often say, '*Anybody can get sober, but it takes work to stay sober once the pink cloud of recovery fades.*' I had long found that statement rather demeaning and dismissive because what is truly happening is that the traumatic symptoms that caused most of us to use in the first place were still there, especially at the body level. For me, those symptoms were primarily dissociative in nature.

Fortunately, one of my graduate professors referred me to a trauma specialist, one of the first to offer EMDR (eye movement desensitization and reprocessing) therapy in earnest in Northeast Ohio. This counselor, also named Janet, was a skillful EMDR therapist and was not easily startled by addiction or dissociation. Using a dissociative experiences scale and a clinical interview, she diagnosed me with what was at the time called Dissociative Disorder Not Otherwise Specified. Between her giving me that diagnosis and a framework for understanding my system of parts, it felt like my whole world suddenly made sense. This treatment was the beginning of another long journey to really recover my mental health, in addition to my sobriety. Yet after experiencing two extended courses of EMDR therapy before I graduated with my master's in 2005, I felt more optimistic about making it—both in recovery, and in my own life.

It is not lost on me how fortunate and privileged I was to have two amazing women who deeply understood both trauma and addiction work with me during these vulnerable years. I am very upset that this kind of care is not available or easily known to the scores of others like me walking around with unhealed trauma, and seeking all the ways that we can dissociate from it quickly and intensely. So much of the work I've done as a professional is to build awareness around trauma-focusing and dissociation-informing addiction care, which is possible regardless of the model you use to treat addiction. Both Janets, decades apart, showed me how trauma knowledge and trauma recovery can work alongside a 12-step program of recovery. Writing this now, over twenty years into my continuous sobriety journey, I identify as having a disease (substance use disorder) that is in remission and as someone whose addiction was a natural progression of a life that had become quite attached to the dissociative state. Dissociation fills us with that elusive sense of ease and comfort.

We have a technical model out there to describe the working tenets of addiction as dissociation, and Adam researched our ideas for his doctoral dissertation toward his PhD, which was officially conferred in 2023. However, in the spirit of "keep it simple" that has come to define my work, let me break it all down for you in summary:

- When children and young people dissociate often, their brains can become bonded to the dissociative state.
- Dissociation feels comfortable and even normal in order to withstand traumatic situations and triggers.
- When drugs, alcohol, or other reinforcing behaviors are introduced, these amplify the already existing experience of dissociation.
- Addictions then become the predominant way of "severing" from the present moment or the self.

- After a period of abstinence or attempt at recovery, it's very common for earlier-in-life dissociative phenomena to reemerge.
- It's imperative for addiction treatment to not just be more trauma-sensitive, but also more dissociation-sensitive.

The most common question we receive when presenting this simple form of the model is "What does it mean to be bonded to the dissociative state, and how does this connect to addiction?" As Adam explained it in his dissertation, primarily citing Nijenhuis and van der Hart's (2011) dissociation in trauma model, being pathologically bonded or "addicted" is by definition the inability to consciously control reentry from the dissociative state or return to a "normal" level of present-day consciousness. The dissociative process impacts aspects of behavior, perception, temporal and spatial awareness, learning (possibly state-dependent or associative learning), memory, motivation, and self. Also, the lack of ability to return to homeostasis makes the dissociative state a state of necessity. Being inappropriately bonded, attached, or addicted is to be in a state of dependence and emotional need.

I chose to write this chapter more as a survivor and less as a professional, even though wisdom from both sides of this adult self hopefully came through. Dissociation is nothing to be afraid of. It is not a dirty word that should automatically set off bells of clinical alarm. For so many of us, it's how we've naturally learned to adapt to early lives full of trauma where we could not escape. And in recovery, we can continue to use many of these gifts of dissociation in the service of our recovery. I believe that my disso-ciative mind helps me navigate the tortuous landscape of modern times and still keep my sanity largely intact . . . without having to drink or take drugs. Even though chocolate cake and brownies can still be a treat in which we overly indulge at time, there is no more hoarding and no more shame in what we eat. And yes, we must constantly monitor our tendencies to overwork when we may really need to just rest and be sad for a while. I am/we are grateful for solid people in our support network today who keep us accountable to putting our health and well-being first, even though it feels like the whole world can depend on us sometimes.

We believe that a life lived out in the open is the best, healthiest, and most adaptive life that we can live for ourselves in the present. As defines so much of our work in the field of dissociation studies, this also means being out in our professional circles as a person with a dissociative system who manages to thrive. We hope that, in some small way, sharing this part of our story here in a collection of sharings from wild and wonderful women may inspire you to be even more open about your journey. And if the time doesn't feel right for that just yet, that's okay, too. We honor your right to heal in your own way and wish you a life free from shame. None of us have to carry it anymore.

References

Marich, J., and A. O'Brien. 2018. "Demystifying Dissociation: A Clinician's Guide." *Addiction Professional* magazine, December 4, 2018. www.psychcongress.com/article/mindful ness-and-psychotherapies/demystifying-dissociation-clinicians-guide.

Nijenhuis, E. R. S., and O. van der Hart. 2011. "Dissociation in Trauma: A New Definition and Comparison with Previous Formulations." *Journal of Trauma and Dissociation* 12 (4): 416–45. https://doi.org/10.1080/15299732.2011. 570592.

O'Brien, A., and Marich, J. 2019. "Addiction as Dissociation: An Emerging Paradigm for Case Conceptualization and Improving Care with Traumatized Populations." Institute for Creative Mindfulness. www.instituteforcreativemindfulness.com/icm-blog-redefine-therapy/addiction-as-dissociation-model-by-adam-obrien-dr-jamie-marich.

O'Brien, A. 2023. "Addiction as Trauma-Related Dissociation: A Phenomenological Investigation of the Addictive State." Doctoral diss., International University for Graduate Studies, 2023.

Chapter 3

Bricolage

On Being Enough—Healing through Narrative Co-construction

Myriam D. (Mimi) Savage, PhD, RDT/BCT

bricolage: the process or technique of creating a new artwork, concept, etc., by appropriating a diverse miscellany of existing materials or sources.
—*Oxford English Dictionary*

Introduction: Bygone Era

The cicadas were noisy where my grandmother's white, metal Maytag wringer washer stood in the grassy backyard next to the kitchen's screen door beside the thriving vegetable garden. On the front porch, I watched with my child eyes the moment a slim, young blond woman wearing a yellow cotton dress rumbled toward us in a shiny and substantial car. She parked it on the red dirt driveway next to my grandparents' wooden house on Peach Street, which was on the other side of the railroad tracks, near the big tobacco barn up the paved road. The young lady stood in front of the house and my grandmother, in her blue housedress, seemed much older as she approached from the backyard where the wringer washer was. She was carrying a wicker laundry

46

basket filled with pressed and neatly stacked linens. The young woman handed my grandmother a dollar with an audible, "Thank you, Sarah," addressing her by her first name as she took the ample basket from outstretched arms. She didn't look my way. My grandmother's honey-brown fingers folded the worn dollar bill handed to her from the lady's freckled hands in half, with a look on her face that appeared to disapprove of the moment and the woman. I hadn't seen that interaction or look before.

Bricolage Fragments

Griot

The following chapter explores the intersections of belonging, othering, its connection to trauma, and my own narrative of the internal struggle of identifying self-worth as a woman of color— and, more specifically, as a Black identifying woman in the world and in the creative art therapy profession of drama therapy. These thematic intersections are all aligned to self-esteem and how others perceive us as women in our social and professional spheres. The intersections affect how we stride on the planet and our overall health. The following exploration bade me to act as a bricoleur, collecting and implementing the odds and ends—fragments of the historical narratives that visit me; creating a collage of images, implementing snippets of stories in order to form a larger landscape of understanding—both for the reader and myself; a free-form approach inviting me to scribe the lived stories that function as examples of our collective vulnerability. Only when I pause, noting and re-collecting the useful threads and seeds, like an invested mama bird building her secure nest through writing, does the story I want to share come through. It is in the collecting, forming, and then sharing of stories from which deep understanding for self and others can occur.

As a parallel process, I share how a creative arts therapeutic action of creating a narrative-based assemblage construction called the Poetic Home exercise can offer personal insight about such things related to self-identity and trauma. Insight exists in the social constructionism approach, in the courageous encounter where the process of making meaning with others leads to self-actualization.

When I ponder the very pregnant and universal topic of self-worth, there are two distinct landscapes embedded in bygone eras that come to mind. This chapter began with the first, a scribed memory of my eight-year-old self experiencing an interaction that illustrates the tone of time, place, and relationship where much of my initial conscious awareness about the circumstances of belonging, self-worth, and othering started. This narrative inquiry praxis looks forward, backward, and considers chronology, place, and the relational through an emic perspective—an auto-ethnographic unpacking that situates lived data in story form for an empathic as well as intellectual understanding.

The upcoming narrative landscapes feature my grandfathers within those bygone eras; both men were worlds apart from each other and yet so precise in the way they strode the planet upon which they thrived—at least when I met them. Afuape (2011) mentions the importance of reclaiming memory, arguing that as a result of the attack on memory that comes with abuse, violence, and oppression, people who experience emotional distress and psychosocial difficulties often experience life as single-storied, predominantly featuring hopelessness and despair. Therefore, reclaiming memory, as I do in the following pages, is a liberatory act and an important part of resisting these felt abuses of power—that may be recent to me or may have occurred generations ago to my ancestors. I am not absolute in knowing how the fragments of my sharing will affect the reader or myself. Nor do I claim the ensuing storied pieces complete the materials for a whole narrative of an entire lifetime. Reclaiming storied and variegated fragments through a bricolage practice (Denzin and Lincoln 2008) of story making and writing here serves as the healing process of tending, mending, and witnessing in the role of the griot, defined as the respected West African narrator of oral traditions, poetry, history, and genealogy, which I hold from my ancestors—a significant interactional aspect of the drama therapist and social constructionist position I embody. In that vein, my hope for this chapter journey is for us to recognize, resonate, reclaim, and regenerate through story—together.

Fragments: Belonging

Both of my grandfathers were storytellers. They were from different continents—one from the French countryside in the Aquitaine, near Bordeaux; a place where stone citadels and aqueducts have existed for centuries surrounded by the rocky soil that grows acres upon acres of thriving grape vines. The other was from the historic rural Black American settlement in Clay County, near the all-White river town of Celina, Tennessee, known as Free Hill, where freed and runaway slaves cohabitated with First Nation people, cultivated the mountain land, and were relatively self-sufficient and mostly free from the violent altercations of White people, even during the Civil War when the state was under Confederate rule. My grandmother, Sarah Hill, was a third-generation descendant of a White woman, Virginia Hill, the daughter of a plantation owner who single-handedly brought her mixed-race slaves from North Carolina to Tennessee, bought 2,000 acres of wooded land, and resided with them for a while until she left it all to them. My orphaned paternal grandfather, Floyd Savage, who had a miserable childhood, met my young grandmother in Free Hill. Their marriage produced eleven children. Grandpa Floyd worked as a camp cook in the rural Appalachian Mountains, where long-bearded White folks had never seen a Black man, and he worked as a sharecropper. He bought land in nearby Kentucky, becoming an elder who counseled people from all walks of life, no matter their background. Walter Floyd Savage was a deacon in the Church of Christ. A civil activist, he served his community and created a home for his family within it despite his childhood and lifelong experience of racism and classism.

My maternal grandfather, Camille Richard, fathered seven children in all. During retirement, he was fond of singing French limericks and painting his stone cottage window shutters multiple striped colors. He was the black sheep of his family of vineyard owners: eccentric and gregarious despite a laryngectomy that didn't stop him from pushing out words from his belly or puffing on the occasional Gauloise cigarette. He loved his wine, even in his soup, and he had served in the military during WWII until he was captured and imprisoned by the Germans as a POW. During the war, my French grandparents were separated from most of their children in the countryside. The children were forced to do vineyard labor as wards of the state during the Nazi occupation of the region. There is a story that after the war, when Camille learned that my mother, who was then a little girl, was in a nearby hospital recovering from jaundice, he tried to break into her room to kidnap her back home, but he was caught and sent away, though my mother stole a glimpse of him in the commotion. Both of my grandfathers followed through on what they thought was the right thing to do in the world, though their hands were often tied by the powers that be.

Why do these memories come to mind as I write about belonging, othering, trauma, and self-worth? What does this history have to do with my position as a drama therapist or as an academic who facilitates and teaches counseling psychology, drama therapy, and expressive arts? The significance of these recounted memories relates to my developing self-identity that pertains to self-worth and its effect on positionality in all the social identities I now hold. Both elders accepted me, as if they were proud of who I was as a person, even when I was a young child and hadn't accomplished much. I didn't make any extra effort to prove to them I was worthy of being noticed, nor had I experienced impostor syndrome from a disbelief of their praise about who or what I was. With that, I also felt a sense of belonging in their environments, even though their worlds were foreign and unfamiliar to me.

Despite my acceptance in the family, that era was a time when not belonging to the majority rule meant one's skin pigment was judged; this not belonging to those in power due to race or being foreign was real and felt on my part and my mother's when I was eight years old. We lived with my grand-parents in Kentucky for a year while my father was in Vietnam during the Tet Offensive—one of the most violent periods American soldiers encountered during the war. I had only just arrived in America from Europe. It was culture shock to live in the States during the civil rights era with my Black family and my White, foreign mother, especially in the small, segregated town of Franklin. Before this we had lived at the California army base where my father was stationed for a year before being deployed. The base was near a beach town where anti-war hippies were professing love and peace, which contrasted greatly to Governor George Wallace's fierce segregationist policies touted throughout Southern states. Living in Franklin meant the loss of a lifestyle that was familiar to me, which was Californian and European.

There existed within me a paradox of belonging to family while, at the same time, not belonging to the world in which I lived in 1968. Feelings of loss comingled with the fear my family felt because of the war. My father was obliged to fight as a career soldier—a situation that was even more pronounced because this was a televised war. We searched for my father's image on the television screen in my grandparents' living room every evening on the nightly news.

Fragments: Acceptance

Grandpa Floyd sat me next to him during monthly Bible study meetings in his living room, requesting I read excerpts aloud from the Old Testament, all the while praising my reading abilities to the gathered elderly audience of his congregation. On those early evenings sitting next to him, I knew I was accepted and felt proud.

In France, over the several years I visited him as a child, Camille—my mother's biological father, whom she searched for and found when she was twenty-one, would drive me around the Blaye countryside in his mini tractor introducing me to his curious neighbors along the way to his shrimping nets in the Gironde estuary, where we stopped to pick chamomile flowers to bring home for tea and where he showed me how he wove and repaired his nets by hand. In those intimate times, I witnessed how delighted and proud he was to call me his own as he shared his interests and skills.

These two adult figures from my childhood were animated, assured, and steadfast in their opinions about the world, about love, acceptance, and their allegiance to others. Perhaps they were steadfast due to the trials and errors of their own making—from which they learned. They were not perfect. I hadn't experienced years of growing up in their company, and I came into their lives during an era when accepting a mixed-race grandchild could be publicly challenging, humiliating for some families, and even dangerous. My parents' lives were threatened several times in America and in Europe because of their interracial union. I was born before Jim Crow was abolished in parts of the U.S. and when children like me were not commonly seen in many parts of the country because marriage between the races in America was illegal until 1967 when the U.S. Supreme Court declared anti-miscegenation state laws were unconstitutional. The law was passed barely a year before my mother and I arrived to live in the small Kentucky town where my father's parents, his youngest brothers, and sister lived.

Fragments: Home

My grandparents were intrinsically connected to their homelands, which included the harvest and farming. This was inherent to their self-sufficiency and belonging to community and the earth. They abided by a calendar of the seasons that bore fruit and crops. Perhaps because Mother Nature was in charge, there existed tolerance, wisdom, and respect about the passing of time and all the conditions of humanity one could encounter in a lifetime. Because of this example of acceptance and embracing something larger than mankind, such as nature, I've often reflected on the concept of belonging to something tremendous like Mother Nature or to a loving community. This is the opposite of *othering*, which can be an intentional practice of making someone feel small and unworthy. I became more conscious of this feeling of othering while in America at my young age, especially in Franklin, from incidents such as discovering the scribble of a racial slander connected to my name in the girls' bathroom stall.

In contrast, I recall a somatic and emotional experience—a distinct feeling of belonging—once while I was with a group of strangers, friends of some friends of mine, who had gathered on a sidewalk after a play-reading we had attended. Ironically, everyone there was taller than me and yet, as I looked up at the small crowd of faces, I felt very connected to them. It was a first feeling for me of belonging to something outside of my family and despite our differences in physical size or family backgrounds, we had phenotype in common. We shared similar hues of melanin, similar hair texture, and a rhythm in conversation. There didn't exist a prerequisite to fulfill, in order for me to fit in and I felt safe and seen—a part of something magnificent. That night, I defined the new sensation I experienced as the feeling of home.

Bricolage: Othering as Trauma

Fragments: Childhood Dissociation as Othering

The dissociative self is born out of trauma, and the ensuing triggers from childhood trauma incidents manifest as the self-fragmentation our brains rely upon so we can function as adults. Childhood trauma can result in a splitting off from parts of the child's developing whole self, enabling dissociation from the harm. The trauma response controls and keeps at bay the encountered harm while preserving a higher-functioning part of the self because the trauma is so overwhelmingly visceral. This response affects our consciousness about the trauma incident. Perhaps the dissociative phenomenon is connected to a form of both externalized and internalized othering—of being left out and fragmented away from a safe, whole base of connection and belonging to oneself and others. My childhood narrative, as a whole, was not entirely secure, though I was loved by my parents. Harmful events compounded with systemic conditions created overwhelm and trauma in my young life.

It is important to fully define what psychological trauma is, considering how much it can affect the feeling of being on the outside of normative existence, leading to an isolative viewpoint and relational dysfunction. Psychological trauma's influence can be seen in various residual psychosocial behaviors and whole-body responses that occur when we perceive real-time, personal, immediate threat or danger. Fight-or-flight survival aims, under threatening and heightened circumstances, rely on basic defense mechanisms so all the parts of the self can be sustained. Banitt (2019, 38) states, "The brain seems to have a divide and conquer strategy to cope with memories that could derail functionality in the mind and body, especially in the early years when the whole brain is still quite plastic."

In this way, my trauma memories from childhood have been compartmentalized; a past fear of drowning, and another of abandonment, for instance. Some memories stem from intentional abuse—of being locked up during preschool in a dark basement cellar behind bars by French nuns when I was three, for instance, an action that sent me into fevered shock. Some actions caused unintentional harm, like being left with strangers at five years old without understanding why my mother was gone; she had been committed to a psychiatric ward. All these trauma incidents, and others involving my identity as a mixed-race child, occurred and were compounded between the ages of three and eight, fulfilling several of the adverse childhood experience (ACE) criteria by a very young age.

Intentional methods of repair with a therapist involve

addressing one or more of three essential components of a trauma incident's psychological and/or bodily manifestations at a time. This could include processing the recurring narrative of the event, which may be devoid of sensory or feeling; or the recurring snapshots, nightmares, or flashbacks steeped in the five senses experienced at the event; or the explicit recurring feeling state derived from the incident (Banitt 2019, 38–40). Trauma processing on parental abandonment occurred for me through feeling state therapy processes, reflected in the following poetry I created several years ago while attending sessions with a Jungian therapist:

Still

A stranger's house
One toy on the floor
Who was I and
Where were they?
Left. Alone.
My head down
    —blurred
I saw feet
    —muddled
I hear voices.
No voice of my own
I sank into
a pool of
    alone
like a penny dropped into a shallow
pond—I watched
the circular motion of
water expand into the obscure
and I was in
    the center

very still.

Processing historical trauma from the split off parts of my five-year-old self meant tending to a fragmented memory that contributed to isolative behavior during my young adult years. Recovery has meant assembling the pieces that connect to loss through creative art therapies and whole-body processes. Perhaps the impetus for doing this for myself and others is why I was attracted to drama and expressive therapies as a profession. Trauma retrieval methods can cause positive lifelong effects because of the way we humans encode memory, with all its systems of ordered parts, which evolve as a person's cognitive and emotional capacity increases. Writing this chapter contributes to the larger quest of making tangible the internalization of such feelings occurring at developmentally susceptible times.

Fragments: Micro- and Macroaggression as Othering

At the root of micro- and macroaggressions are systems of oppression or individual subversive, aggressive behaviors that are intentionally or unintentionally set against, for instance, people of color. This occurs when dominant populations project their own feelings of inferiority onto a group of people and proceed to use that projection in order to justify their supremacist acts. Some examples of inane microaggressive behavior I have experienced might put this into perspective for the reader or may resonate with lived experience. With obvious, outward surprise by the interrogating person, I've been asked how does someone like me (meaning a person who looks like me) ever get accepted to an Ivy League university. I've been approached by White women who, out of the blue, want to pet my hair because of their own fascination with something unusual to them, which is objectifying to say the least. People have expressed surprise that I speak so "eloquently"—code for judging level of intelligence. Someone once remarked it must've been hard for my father to get out of the ghetto, though he never lived in one. But if he had, why would he *need* to get out per some other person's opinion or assumptions? A White nun at my Catholic high school wrote on my report card that she was concerned as to why I was working so hard in her class, achieving high marks—as if it was unnatural for me to strive. She hadn't considered my drive was resultant of historical poverty, racism, classism, and even the immigrant's dream to succeed. She never investigated why my parents placed me in the school; the several incidents when I was called the "n" word by her students; nor fathomed how, culturally, I was programmed to earn, achieve, and be as good, if not better than, my privileged peers so that there would be less of an excuse to fail me or label me as inadequate due to my race or background. Microaggression existed during the 1970s, though no one labeled it as such.

I mention the compounding micro- and macroaggressions that people of color regularly encounter not to illustrate victim-ization but rather resilience. People of color tolerate these seemingly innocuous or often overtly aggressive interactions regularly due to implicit or explicit biases from people who do not see their likeness in others, with the wonderful bell hooks (2010, 100) suggesting that beginning with interactional educa-tion and community we can make change: "We must teach students to first see that perspectives vary depending on the degree to which any of us have been socialized to have blind spots in our thinking based on race, gender, and class."

Individually experienced, or as a community, continual micro- and macroaggressions can emotionally exhaust the recipients and negatively affect their mental and physical health over time. Granted, all humans suffer and experience loss that can cause trauma. Hegemony in America, however, mechanizes marginalization and othering through systemic oppression via limiting, inequitable sociopolitical practices involving policing, employment, redlining, voting, and housing, as well as medical and education access. These mechanisms of privilege exclude populations of people based on gender identity, sexual orientation, age, physical ability, illness, neurodiversity, physical size, religion, race, ethnicity, class, and language. These people are then affected by the social determinants of othering, which challenges their sense of self-worth on any given day. That lowered sense of self-worth almost certainly influences how the less privileged person handles trauma in mind and body, consciously and unconsciously.

Fragments: Historical Trauma as Othering

We can look to historic events, and even the recent sobering Black doll experiments (Tjandra 2021), to realize the consequences of societal implicit and explicit biases placed upon Black and Brown children, which detrimentally affect their self-esteem even into adulthood. Poor self-esteem has lasting psychological and physical effects on a person, which has been definitively shown by the landmark Adverse Childhood Experiences (ACE) Study (CDC 2023). A collective meta understanding about which group has been at the top of the social, economic, class, and race ladders—thereby comprehending how status works due to the history of colonization in a capitalist country—is essential in order to create a level playing field for marginalized people. Kimmel (2006, as cited by Afuape 2011, 112) makes an analogy about supremacy as it is connected to belonging, remarking if you are a White person you are "everywhere you look. You are the standard against which everything and everybody else is measured." Furthering the point, he states: "Any college course that does not have the word woman, or gay or minority in the title is, de facto, a course about men, heterosexuals, and White people. But we call those courses literature, history, or political science."

Imagine a lifetime realizing that the environment where you are educated, the books you are learning from, and the spaces where you socialize and learn about politics, history, and personal relationships are dominated by a culture that doesn't recognize your historical and present worth, centering truth only on White, male, Western European history. If you are a Black identifying person, or from any other marginalized group who is educated in the Western world, in order to be considered intelligent, accepted, and worthy of employment, you are most often subjected to environments devoid of materials that represent your personhood and culture. Most likely, your education consisted of an absence of the people who look like you, who are reflected back to you. The dominant world controlled the narratives, erasing most of what historically defines you and an entire group of citizens who should be honored as major cultural, intellectual, and physical contributors to the country in which you reside. Historically, the impact of micro- and macroaggressions has been substantial and continues, although the youngest generation of BIPOC and marginalized folx these days (depending on where in the world a person resides) may be more able to benefit from the support and positive impact of historically Black colleges and universities (HBCUs) and other community and educational organizations. Still, instances of inequality exist. One example of recent research shows Black women in the U.S. being three times more likely to die from pregnancy-related causes than White women, partly due to variations of healthcare, underlying chronic conditions, structural racism, and implicit bias (CDC 2023).

Bricolage: Responsibility

Fragments: Resilience

Sociologist Johnson (2006) posits social justice is based on action stemming from self-reflection and from understanding what privilege is and what it's got to do with each of us. He notes that progress means seeing ourselves as part of the process of change toward something better. His stance is to embrace difference by nurturing his own responsibility, even though he was not directly responsible for inventing the legacy of privileged identity that was passed on to him as a White, heterosexual, nondisabled male when he was born into this society. The knowledge and definition of privilege for me begins with unraveling personal childhood narratives. When my grandfather, a deacon, entered through the Catholic church doors during mass for my First Communion in Franklin, I could see his discomfort and courage. I noticed White faces turning to look at him from the pews as he took his seat beside me and my mother. There weren't any Black parishioners, and this was not his Church of Christ congregation. It was 1968, and evidently, we stood out, a reminder of being in a world designed for a dominating majority. This rule was connected to something obvious I noticed when I held my mother's hand in public places in Kentucky. Privilege for me as a mixed-race child or Black identifying person would've meant that none of these public mother-child affectionate interactions would feel wounding. None of the verbal and emotional defenses I built up to explain my mother's accent or attempts at conversation with White, and some Black, people when she was with me would've provoked discomfort if things were fair. Equal rights would've meant that such encounters would've been respectful, and people would have engaged with us without dominance, disdain, or fear.

An inherent and modeled ability was awakened in me during this period that recognizes an attribute of African American spirituality, referred to as survival theology (Black and Rubenstein 2009), which finds life's meaning amid suffering and seeks justice from sociopolitical oppression while doing good and God's work in community. This was very much my grandfather Floyd's resilient stance as he entered the all-White Catholic church that day and one that I have respected. Survival theology was handed down from times of slavery and, in this case, from the time my relatives were harbored on Free Hill, a community of freed slaves established in Tennessee before the Civil War.

Fragments: Skid Row

Several years ago, I was contracted by a documentary filmmaker Alina Skrzeszewska for her film *Game Girls*; she asked me to facilitate free drama therapy workshops for unhoused women, which she filmed in a Skid Row storefront in Los Angeles. Women and families were a growing unhoused population there at the time; within fifty city blocks (0.4 square miles) of downtown Los Angeles terrain, over half the area's 4,000 people were living unsheltered. The film's focus was on women and their strengths amid their unhoused challenges. Through flyers and contacts with shelters, food banks, social workers, and Skid Row community organizers, we invited women to meet weekly for drama therapy groups for the better part of three years, creating community through an open-door policy of group interaction that featured the women's interests and socioemotional needs at the time. Outside the filmed work-shop sessions, life was still happening with deaths, marriages, addiction, sobriety, abuses, successes, lots of loss, and the conse-quences of systemic socioeconomic inequities and intergenera-tional trauma, which were also documented—the collective and individual experiences of life on Skid Row.

On the first day I encountered the women, I was nervous, even though I had facilitated thousands of groups in psychiatric units, schools, and clinics. A middle-aged woman, like others in the room, carried her belongings in a rolling cart that held several plastic bags. She parked it in the corner of the storefront room. I approached her, remarking and complementing how fit her arms were. She snapped back, stating they were an outcome of carrying her belongings daily on the streets in search of shelter and food. I understood, in that moment, the anger she felt toward me. I was privileged and out of ignorance had the nerve to compliment her on circumstances that were harming her—being unhoused and struggling to keep what little she had on her person for fear of being robbed, of losing her identity, and the remaining possessions she owned.

The women who converged every Thursday afternoon were mostly Black and Latinx, with everyone experiencing abuse: namely economic, domestic, childhood, and systems abuse. When I began, I assumed the social and economic differ-ences between us would be uncomfortable because I owned a house and lived with my family. I didn't foresee that my own life experiences would act as a catalyst of discourse between us as women. I held shame around my privileges, though my mother was once a ward of the state like many of them and had been unhoused during her early twenties in France. Dominant society and media often judge the unhoused as being less worthy and on the fringes of the productive world. When I set foot in the storefront, hearing sirens blaring in the neighborhood surrounded by daily violence, I made a point of down-playing any of my personal successes. Eventually though, it was this awareness of my privilege (Afuape 2011) that permitted me to really see and hear the women's narratives more clearly.

I followed the dictum of being intentional about creating culture while facilitating it, which meant I also had to find the brave spaces that I was asking the women to find (Brown 2021, 53). Although there were differences between us, the prevalent message that grew from our mutual encounters was our commonality: success and loss, hope and strength. They taught me how they experienced "home" in deep and resilient ways. There was not a definitive line separating us when it came to our mutual historical trauma around systemic racism, poverty, and the rights to citizenship, or our complex trauma histories that pertained to family loss. Our harmed parentages, and for many of us, our enslaved ancestors, provided the bond of mutual aid. As women or as mothers, whether a person was transgender or cisgender, together we recognized each other, navigated discomfort, celebrated triumphs, mourned losses, and tended to mental illness as well as PTSD.

Fragments: Life Lessons

There are life lessons learned on Skid Row—on what it is like being on the outside while working hard to be on the inside of self-acceptance and feeling safe. Condemnation is set upon marginalized folx by a ruling class that attempts to enforce an internalized message of shame. Was it shame my grandfather was supposed to feel when he came to my First Communion or when I held my mother's hand in that town in 1968? I have learned as a biracial woman and as an academic and drama therapist who has internalized certain societal messages—spoken or unspoken—that success in our hegemonic United

States can most often mean proving to strangers, and yourself, that you are worthy. This takes enormous and ongoing endurance that is often handed down to us generationally in accordance to our culture. Culture and not just family history must also be considered as the instigator of trauma for people (Afuape 2011). Societal messages about acquiring success may be related to feeling less than good enough for much of the time one is striving hard to grab the brass ring—at least in the context of some of my own personal striving and goal setting. I can speak to my own Afrocentric and immigrant-influenced cultural upbringing, which obliges me to be strong, persevere, and do well, despite my own trauma landscape. Where does this urge to prove myself live in my body? Why is it part of how I stride on the landscape of my life? How does it affect my sense of being enough for myself?

Bricolage Construction: A Poetic Home

Fragments: All the Pieces of a Whole

The preceding questions are the prompts for a drama therapy exercise I designed and facilitated in response to self-preservation for the individual who is experiencing loss of self, loss as part of societal stigmatization, loss of connection to others—all in the name of tending to one's reclaim on being enough. The drama therapy exercise called the Poetic Home was inspired by artist Brigid Collins's work and modeled after narradrama techniques (Dunne 2006), a method of drama therapy using narrative therapy constructs. This exercise asks the participant to create a container in which to place their thoughts and feelings, "a home base for a personal, healing narrative" (Savage 2015). I had noticed the vicarious trauma the *Game Girls* documentary crew experienced on Skid Row—affecting their emotional health due to witnessing tragic narratives via camera and sound work, a form of compassion stress. I developed this exercise and explored it with them and various groups of therapists, students, and clients, working first with written words or with a visual image they drew, inspired from being listened to and from being witnessed and mirrored within a projective therapy method of distancing them from a problem-saturated challenge.

The interdisciplinary, experiential, developmental, and intermedial method of opening space through action-based creative exercises is helpful as participants get to re-story a problem-saturated self-narrative, such as feeling as if they are inadequate. It offers perspective via a three-dimensional and full-body interaction through the participant's deconstruction and reconstruction of an eight-by-eight-inch cardboard box that will eventually represent a symbolic preferred narrative. Some of narradrama's therapeutic aims in this exercise are

- warming up to new descriptions of self-identity and/or the environment
- externalizing problems by using projective techniques
- exploring personal agency, and
- creating closure through witnessed rituals and reflective teams (Dunne 2006, 42).

From leading the Poetic Home exercise, I've observed that the small world of a box offers entrance to a bigger narrative for both client and therapist (Savage 2015). This occurred for various participants contending with loss, identity crises, and self-care who titled their Poetic Homes variously as "Illumi-nalchemy; Ephemeral; Home; Window; Nest; Learning Ways of Knowing; Un-American Fake Dream; The Healing Light of Flow; Balanced Chaos" (Savage 2015), as well as: "It Was

Silent; Negative Space/Rupture; Freedom/Control; Don't Cross the Line." For instance, a *Game Girl* crew member made several tableaux from the eight-by-eight cardboard box they were given, cutting into side walls, pasting magazine images on them, drizzling glue for texture, and re-constructing it all into varied panoramic stories. She stated afterward, "For me its power truly revealed itself in the group context . . . The open box corresponded to my approach of letting things pass through me and to fly through landscapes, stories, lives, without a prede-termined structure." Another person shared: "I have a hard time fixing boundaries. And this time I felt I needed to protect myself from the overwhelming emotions floating during the workshops. So, yes, my house would be about protection" (Savage 2015; participants' personal conversations, January 2014).

The six steps to construct a Poetic Home ideally occur through dyadic work within a larger workshop community with processing aims of healing and dispelling negative self-defi-nitions.

1. Pick a partner and discuss self-care issues, challenges, dangers, transferences, and counter-transferences—all the topics of what being enough may be for you.
2. After discussion, *make response art* by doodling or drawing on paper what was shared. How does your self-care appear visually? Discuss further, while partners scribe descriptive words that come up.
3. Use *imaginal dialogue* (McNiff 2008) to make fluid sculptures that explore what the response art looks like in the body (include the voice), and create a moving sculpture of your partner's self-care art response from the previous discussion. Refer to the

art image, interpret it, and bring to life as many aspects as possible of the image and the narrative you witnessed; a playback response.

4. *Discuss* the experience. Check in with your partner about how the embodied doubling fits their experience. Switch roles and repeat.

5. *Scavenge objects* and potential craft materials outside in nature and/or the interior of the workshop space. Using art materials provided, implement the words you discovered from literature, your own poetry, or initial shared response art. Collect elements *to assemble an image of preferred self-identity and care* informing you that you are enough.

6. Reflect on the process. Group leader invites sharing, discussion of the process in the larger group. The Poetic Home acts as a transitional object you can take with you from the shared, witnessed experience.

Poetic Bricolage: Emergent Construction

The Urban Dictionary defines *poetic* as a person's self-expression. Being poetic is turning little things that no one would see right away into novel meaning, such as fashioning a simple container to hold a preferred self-portrait through the construction of the Poetic Home or the construction of this very chapter. Poetry may be witnessed in the fragments, bits, and pieces that reside on these pages. My intention is to share stories as a bold, individually, and socially constructive action. Awareness is built upon this relational interaction; the messiness of it all is an invitation toward finding congruency of the dissociative fragmentations caused by historical and childhood trauma. In community, through an exchange of personal story, we may be able to recognize ourselves and others in response to the effects of othering, aggression, and heightened fear by embracing a less dominant and androcentric model than fight, flight, or freeze (Afuape 2011, 214). There needs to be the healing opportunity to affiliate with others and seek generative social support, through a sentient option to flock (Ebersohn 2012) and gather, which women have instinctively done for thousands of years—just as we are now doing within these pages, in an act of emergent construction through sharing.

References

Afuape, T. 2011. *Power, Resistance and Liberation in Therapy with Survivors of Trauma: To Have Our Hearts Broken.* London: Routledge.

Banitt, S. P. 2019. *Wisdom, Attachment, and Love in Trauma Therapy: Beyond Evidence-Based Practice.* New York: Routledge.

Black, H. K., and R. L. Rubenstein. 2009. "The Effect of Suffering on Generativity: Accounts of Elderly African American Men." *Journals of Gerontology, Series B* 64B, no. 2 (March): 296–303. https://doi.org/10.1093/geronb/gbn012.

Brown, A. M. (2021). *Holding Change: The Way of Emergent Strategy Facilitation and Mediation.* Chico, CA: AK Press.

Centers for Disease Control and Prevention. April 2023. "Working Together to Reduce Black Maternal Mortality." www.cdc.gov/healthequity/features/maternal-mortality/index.html.

Denzin, N. K., and Y. S. Lincoln. 2008. *Strategies of Qualitative Inquiry.* Thousand Oaks, CA: Sage.

Dunne, P. 2006. *The Narrative Therapist and the Arts*, 2nd edition. Los Angeles: Possibilities Press.

Ebersohn, L. 2012. "Adding "Flock to 'Fight and Flight': A Honeycomb of Resilience Where Supply of Relationships Meets Demand for Support." *Journal of Psychology* 22 (1): 29–42. https://doi.org/10.1080/14330237.2012.10874518.

Centers for Disease Control and Prevention. 2023. "Fast Facts: Preventing Adverse Childhood Experiences." www.cdc.gov/violenceprevention/aces/fastfact.html.

hooks, b. 2010. *Teaching Critical Thinking: Practical Wisdom*. New York: Routledge.

Johnson, A. G. 2006. *Privilege, Power, and Difference*, 2nd edition. New York: McGraw Hill.

Kimmel, M. 2006. "Toward a Pedagogy of the Oppressor." In *Progressive Black Masculinities*, edited by A. D. Mutua, 64. New York: Routledge.

McNiff, S. 2008. "Imaginal Dialogue in Research, Artwork, and Art Therapy." In *Handbook of the Arts in Qualitative Research: Perspectives, Methodologies, Examples, and Issues*, edited by G. Knowles and A. L. Cole, 29–41. Thousand Oaks, CA: Sage.

Oxford English Dictionary. s/v "bricolage." Accessed October 24, 2023. www.oed.com/dictionary/bricolage_n/.

Savage, M. 2015. "Making Poem Houses as a Drama Therapy Method of Self-Care." *Dramascope* (blog), July 16, 2015. Accessed September 1, 2023. https://thedramascope.wordpress.com/2015/07/16/making-poem-houses-as-a-drama-therapy-method-of-self-care.

Tjandra, K. 2021. "Science, Civil Rights, and the Doll Test." *Peaceful Science*, February 12, 2021. Accessed September 1, 2023. https://peacefulscience.org/articles/science-civil-rights-and-the-doll-test.

Chapter 4

Healing from Sexual Abuse
Robin Shapiro, LICSW

Our culture has an epidemic of sexual abuse and sexual assault. One out of five girls and one out of ten boys have been sexually abused. Most of the abusers are males. Most of the abusers are family members: fathers, brothers, uncles, grandfathers, and stepfathers. Other abusers are usually trusted elders in positions of power: teachers, clergy, doctors, coaches. Some children are sexually trafficked. Their bodies are sold to make money or garner favor for whoever is doing it. Or they're in a cult, often religiously based, where they are sexually available to every male in the family, church, or organization.

Let's be clear: Sex abuse is rape. Children cannot consent to sex. Adults or older children who put younger children in sexual situations are committing sexual assault, and sexual abuse has bad consequences for the survivors.

If the abuse happened just one or two times, the survivor will usually have post-traumatic stress disorder (PTSD), including flashbacks that make it feel like it's happening again, nightmares, a sense of shame, and a lack of trust. Sometimes the PTSD is so bad that the survivor may consider or attempt suicide to stop the sensations and emotions that arise. PTSD may dissipate and then show up again when triggered by dealing with the rapist, or being in a chosen sexual situation, or even reading or watching media with sexual situations.

Survivors often carry guilt or shame from the abuse. Children often think that they deserved and must have caused whatever happened to them. Kids are wired to be adored. If the parents are not able to do that, the child thinks it's because they're not good enough. If a therapy client has been emotionally, physically, or sexually abused, their inner child belief system "knows" that they caused it with their badness. The alternative is to accept that they had no control, which is way too scary! "I should have stopped it! Why did I let that (much older and larger) person do that to me?"

More shame comes from the culture. If the survivor comes from a religious background in which sex outside marriage is "evil," then they may feel "bad" or "iniquitous" for having been "ruined." Part of the cultural problem is that there's little talk or publication of the frequency of sexual abuse, so that survivors often feel isolated in their "differentness."

Survivors can become very codependent. If they were not allowed to say no in their childhoods, they do not know how to say no in their current lives, in sexual and nonsexual situations. They may only see others' needs, completely neglecting their own, or they may be the opposite: completely avoidant of any relationship, because no one can be trusted. They may be connected with people but absolutely mistrustful of what others do or say, since they had no experience of protection or safe connection.

If the abuse happened more than a couple of times or regularly, the survivor is likely to have PTSD and some form of dissociation. Dissociation happens when our nervous system can't tolerate a big physical or emotional feeling. When the pain is too much, our body knocks out the neural network that holds it and brings up another one to cope. Some dissociation involves spacing out, some involves a shift of attention to another topic, and sometimes dissociation involves a new "part" of us coming up that may have no connection or knowledge of the pain. This part arises to take care of business so that we can function. If a person has had a lot of abuse, they may have many parts that arise to deal with both the instances of abuse and the need to function despite the abuse. There will be other parts, often repressed, that carry the memories and pain of the abuse. The majority of people with dissociative identity disorder, which used to be called multiple personality disorder, are survivors of childhood sexual abuse.

Coping with Sexual Abuse

Because of the cultural silence around abuse, and the shame that comes with it, survivors are often reluctant to disclose what happened to them. In order to heal, it's necessary to connect with people who understand the issue. There are dozens of online forums for survivors where people can connect and discuss what happened and learn some coping skills. Many of them are listed on a great website, the National Sexual Violence Resource Center (www.nsvrc.org). Hearing other people's stories helps mitigate the shame of the events: "If it's not their fault, how could it be my fault?" It also normalizes the PTSD, sexual issues, and avoidance of connection that plague many survivors.

If people are experiencing ongoing PTSD, shame, relationship avoidance, and, especially, dissociation, they need to find good psychotherapy. There are two components to good therapy: the kind of therapy it is, and the kind of person doing it. Both are extremely important for survivors' outcomes.

Therapy for Sexual Abuse Survivors

As in any therapy, the therapist must be safe, connectible, and give permission for the client to discuss anything and feel everything. The goals of therapy are

- To rid the client of PTSD, shame, and dissociation around sex abuse, and everything else the client may have suffered
- To help the client develop good boundaries, sexual and otherwise, with all other humans
- That the client can have a healthy, fun, connected sexual relationship, if they want one

The length of therapy depends on who the client is, what happened to them, and what diagnoses they carry. If the person had a good childhood with healthy, loving attachment and one or two sexual assaults by people outside of the family, they may be done in six weeks of a good trauma therapy: EMDR, somatic therapy, and/or ego state work. In EMDR or ego state therapy, the adult part of the client sweetly brings the distressed child up to the present as many times as it takes for the child part to arrive fully in this moment, far removed from the abuse. This healing can be rapid and complete, allowing the client to carry on with her adult life.

If the client was abused by someone close to them, and especially if it happened many times, the client will likely have developed complex PTSD. The client will have deep neural networks of

- Trauma memories or avoidance of the trauma memories
- Overwhelming emotions or avoidance of emotions

- Overdependence or absolute fear of intimacy and dependence
- Constant fear, especially of sexual situations, or sexual acting out

All of these can underlie chronic or acute suicidal ideation.

Some of these clients can have parts that carry all these issues, but separated into deeper, non-overlapping neural networks. If the client was abused in a cult, or in sex trafficking, the parts may have even deeper separations and may have been intentionally programmed for obedience and deference to whoever is in charge. These clients with dissociative identity disorder are healable. It may take years to do all the work and get all parts into the current time and place, knowing the abuse is over, and allowing the most adult part of self to be completely present here and now.

Choosing a Therapist

To choose a good therapist, find someone you can like, trust, and connect with. The therapist must be able to listen to you, and to be able to direct you into the trauma work, even when you want to avoid it. Humor is great, when you know you're being laughed with, not laughed at. The therapist must know therapies that work with trauma. They must have some training and skill in working with abuse survivors.

In my forty-one years of working with survivors of sexual abuse, I've found three kinds of therapies the most helpful. Like all good trauma therapies, they depend on a dual attention: the client is clearly focused in the present, in their most adult part, and somehow connecting with the trauma, while the mechanisms of the therapies clear the distressing event, flashbacks, or sensations.

EMDR (eye movement desensitization and reprocessing) is a sometimes-miraculous method that can clear simple, one-time traumas in a few sessions. It involves the client holding the trauma in mind and body while putting pressure on the memory networks by moving their eyes quickly, or feeling bilateral tapping or pulsing, or hearing bilateral sounds. When I learned it in 1993, several clients who I'd worked with for years to help them cope with the effects of abuse cleared the trauma completely and left therapy within weeks. (I was worried about my income, but then they sent me all their friends!) There are two new forms of EMDR that work even faster. One is EMDR 2.0 (de Jongh 2020), which adds tapping, footsteps, and counting or spelling to the "pressures" on the memory network. It is especially useful with dissociative clients, since clients' brains are too busy trying to attend to four or five different tasks for them to shift into another state. The other is the flash technique (Manfield 2019), which gets clients to strongly focus on a positive memory and storing away the trauma in a "container," while having bilateral stimulation and periodically blinking when told to "Flash!" This technique is great for avoidant clients because they don't have to focus on the distressing event in order to clear it. Both of these two techniques work remarkably well, and often much better than traditional EMDR to move trauma.

Ego state therapy involves establishing a very clear, strong, adult, present-oriented self while connecting to other parts that may carry the trauma or actions of protection against recalling the trauma or being hurt again. There are ways to use simple ego state work to "send" the present-time adult back to the past to rescue the abused self from the abuser and the dangerous past. I've done this with clients' traumas from last week, last year, and forty years ago. (With all of these, you repeat it until there is no fear or other signs of PTSD left in the client.) Ego state therapy is mandatory for work with highly dissociated clients, since it's the only way to organize the clients' parts, and eventually clear their trauma.

Somatic therapies involve connecting people with their safe, strong, present body, then with the old sensations and emotions of the trauma, and with increased awareness sensing or moving through the old bodily experiences of abuse, into the new safe, strong time and body. Do your feet reach all the way to the floor? Were they that long when you were being abused (at five years old)? If your thirteen-year-old abuser attacked you now, could you defend yourself? Feel that adult strength, right now. While you feel your adult body, let's think about that kid and what happened, keeping both in mind.

Many therapists use a combination of two or all three of these therapies to work with trauma survivors to keep the necessary dual attention, groundedness, and pressure on their memory networks for the trauma to clear. Many books and trainings combine these methods. Most therapists have a list of their techniques on their websites, so it's easy to find that information out.

Good therapy includes feeling supported, doing trauma work, and some focus on changes in the here and now. If you've never been able to say "no" or "I want" to anyone, good therapy will give those skills. If you've never had a good sex life, because you spaced out or had a flashback every time you were in a sexual situation, good therapy will help you learn how to say "yes," "no," and "I want" to your sexual partner while staying in the room with that person, without flashing back to the abuse situation. If you've been afraid and avoidant of trusting anyone, a good therapist will give you the experience of a safe person to trust and help you figure out your criteria for a safe and sane partner. Therapists do make mistakes, and a good one will give you a good apology, which builds even more trust.

Sexual Issues for Survivors

The worse and more frequent the sexual abuse was, the more it can mess up adult sexual relationships. Survivors often have flashbacks or dissociation when trying to have good adult sex. Some people feel too frozen to stay in the "zone" of attachment and arousal. Some people space out completely. Some people can't say "no" to what they don't want. And some can't ever say "yes" and have no adult sex life.

A healthy sex life includes both partners being in full consent of whatever happens, both partners being able to say what they want or don't want in any moment, and both partners being fully present and connected with each other through the duration of the sexual encounter. In order to have good sex, a survivor needs to clearly know and feel the difference between the abuser and the chosen lover, and the difference between their little-girl, unable-to-consent self and their adult, sexually mature self. A survivor has to be present enough and clear enough to be able to say "no" or "I want," at any time. (If there's no "no," there's never really a "yes.") She has to be able to say, "I'm thinking about the abuse. I need to take a break, until I'm back in this room with you."

Some survivors start feeling shame the moment they're aroused, because the friction of the original abuse created unwanted arousal. Some survivors go into fear or rage that belong to the abuse time. These people need to get some trauma therapy to heal these old distresses. Some get into B&D or S&M relationships to either reenact their past or to take the opposite, in-control role in it. Sometimes, when the trauma is cleared, they drop the need for these roles. Sometimes, when the trauma is cleared, they are able to do them with more relish.

Some women have no idea what they want sexually. They never have had an orgasm. They never masturbate because any thought of sex brings up abuse. Some of these women just allow their partner to do whatever the partner wants, with no input from them. Often, after the trauma therapy has done its work, these people want to have a good sex life. The first thing they need to know is what they like. There is a nice website, OMGYES.com, that shows graphic videos of a woman's hand on her vulva, and many other first-person videos, and explains pleasure and how to maintain it. A nice book is *For Yourself: The Fulfillment of Female Sexuality* (Barbach 2002). Knowing what you want and then communicating it to your partner is the most important thing. (Aside from choosing a partner who wants those communications!)

Supporting Someone Who Was Sexually Abused

- Let them know it's okay for them talk to about it with you, but that you won't pry.
- If they don't have a good therapist, help them find one.
- Have them look at this chapter if they need resources.
- Normalize it, without minimizing it: "I'm so sorry this happened to you. And you are *so* not the only one. This has happened to about 20 percent of women. It always sucks!"

A person who has successfully recovered from sexual abuse is present, has no flashbacks, is able to happily connect with good people, and is able to assert themselves, saying "yes" and "I want" and "no" at will. They can feel sexual feelings without fear or shame. They can ask for exactly what they want in a sexual situation, including saying "no."

Therapy Stories

Editor's note: The first two cases below are composites drawn from multiple clients; the third is a true story shared with permission with the name changed. Any identifying information has been hidden. Trigger warning: These stories include graphic descriptions of abuse. Please take care of yourself as needed while reading.

Sara: A one-time attack

When Sara was five she stayed at her cousins' house at least once a month. Her girl cousin was just her age. Her two boy cousins were eleven and thirteen years old. The kids were not supervised. They hung out in the basement where the toys, the television, and the train set were, or roamed the neighborhood together or in pairs. They used to wrestle, and Sara got used to being pinned down, but never hurt.

One time, her thirteen-year-old cousin pinned her down, lay down on her, and started rubbing himself against her. Sara was curious and asked him what he was doing.

"What grownups do." *Why?* "Because they like it." *Why?* "Because it feels good." *I don't like it! Stop!* He didn't stop and kept rubbing himself on her until he orgasmed. After that, Sara wouldn't play with him anymore and was quite avoidant of physical contact with boys.

Thirty years later, Sara came to therapy after a bad divorce, to grieve and learn how to move on. In an early session, I asked her if she'd ever experienced physical, emotional, or sexual abuse. She told me about the time with her cousin. When I asked her how she felt, now, when she thought about that incident, she said, "A little scared and a little disgusted." When do these feelings show up now? "When I think about my cousin, and when there's a man on top of me, even when I want him."

We did EMDR with ego state therapy with a focus on the body feelings and emotions:

"Sara, how old are you now?" *Thirty-five.*

"How tall are you?" *Five-foot-six.*

"Would you be able to protect yourself from a horny thirteen-year-old boy, now?" *Absolutely!*

"I want you to find that five-year-old you who is stuck on that floor with that cousin and bring her up here. You hold that girl, letting her know she's safe, and you can protect her . . . Now you and she look at that scene. What's the feeling?" *Confusion and fear.*

"Where are you feeling it?" *In my chest and my throat?*

"How big is it, zero to ten?" *Eight.*

We did eye movements, tapping, and alternating beeps in her ears. The number went down to five, then two, then zero.

"Now think about that event, and what do you notice?" *It seems far away, and my body isn't doing anything.*

"Is it over?" *Finally!*

"What feeling goes with that?" *Relief!*

"Notice where that feeling is in your body, and let's slowly tap that in!"

Three sessions later, after working with some of her relationship issues and doing some work around healthy adult sex, we were done! If she'd had more abuse and an otherwise rotten childhood, it would have taken much longer.

Janet: Early Childhood Incest

Janet was four when her parents split up. When she stayed at her father's house, she stayed in his bed. He was not much of a talker or very attentive. She went to bed first. He would get in bed later and cuddle up against her, which she looked forward to. After a few months, he would begin to stroke her body, which felt good. Then he touched her genitals. And then he started to rub his penis up against her body and especially her behind and her genitals. Things would get more intense, each time, until his orgasm. Then he would wipe them both off and cuddle her to sleep.

This went on until Janet told her mom, asking her, "What is daddy doing when he rubs his thing on me? I kind of like it, but I kind of don't like it." Her mother called her father, told him off, and told him that Janet would never sleep over again, or see him without another adult present.

Janet was devastated. It was the only attention she got from him. When she came to therapy at twenty-six, she had many feelings about it: anger at her father, shame that somehow she had "wanted it," distress that anytime she was with a man she thought about it, and flashbacks and dreams of those interactions with her father.

Therapy started with her and me connecting. We made strong eye contact. I was very responsive to every feeling and thought and sensation that she disclosed. "I feel your sadness. What's it like for you to know how angry and sad I am that you have to deal with this now?"

When I knew we were well connected, we started on the trauma. First, we targeted shame with some ego state work.

"If this had happened to me when I was four, would you think it was my fault?" *No way!*

I explained that all children think that they cause their lives, because it would be too scary to think that they didn't have control. She nodded.

"So, take your grown-up twenty-six-year-old-self back there and get that kid. Introduce yourself to that kid and let her know that you're her grown-up. Bring her up to this office. You and she watch a video of what happened with your dad. What does she see?" *It was her fault. She looked forward to the attention.*

"Given what you said to me about it not being my fault, what does your adult see?" *She was four, it couldn't be her fault!*

"Turn that kid around and look at her with your loving eyes. Tell her exactly what I'm telling you: *Sweetie, it was never your fault. Your dad was a grown-up. You were just a little girl. You didn't even know what he was doing to you. I'm a grown-up now, and I understand good touch and bad touch and I'll decide who gets to touch us, and who doesn't, and how they do that.*"

For about fifteen more sessions, we did EMDR on the anger, disgust, and grief that arose from those times with her father, and then without him. She was able to see his social deficits, and that he was using her, a child, for his unmet needs, and his lack of social acumen. She left therapy feeling present, no longer having flashbacks, able to pursue an adult sexual relationship, and reconciled to having a broken dad of limited capacity.

Lila: Chronic Childhood Sexual Abuse

Lila had a distressing yet all too common story in the world of sexual abuse therapy. When she was two or three, her father started sexually abusing her with full-on penetration. She learned to dissociate the minute he approached her bed. She had dissociated into two parts: the spaced-out abused girl part, and the out-in-the-world, functional part. At thirty-five she came to therapy. She worked. She had a few friends. She avoided relationships and didn't really trust people. And she was starting to get flashbacks from the abuse.

It took many weeks for her to trust me enough to go deep into the work. The work was our relationship, calming exercises, and getting her present with some meditation and other ways to have choices about what she experienced.

About three months in, I asked her to notice a feeling that I could sense in her. She was able to stay with it, identify it as fear, and then explicitly remember her father abusing her at eight years old. We worked to keep her in the safe present: "Notice! Do your feet reach all the way to the ground now? Did they then? Is your father in the room? Are you safe now? . . . Good!"

When we could do that easily, we started the trauma processing with EMDR and ego state therapies. A year later, we had cleared all the sexual abuse. A year after that, we had conquered her reflexive avoidance of closeness. Therapy ended with her dating a good guy, huge relief, and gratitude on both our parts.

Brenda: Early Childhood Gang Rape and Ritual Abuse

At four years old, Brenda was brought to an alleged childcare facility while her parents went to work for an overseas oil company. Her mother brought her into the lobby and hugged her goodbye. The front desk people said they'd take great care of her, directed her to walk through a door, at which point thirteen men in black cowls grabbed her, put her on an altar/table, and brutally raped her. This continued, with different kinds of rituals, for five months.

When I met and evaluated Brenda thirty-five years later, she was clearly living with dissociative identity disorder. She would switch from one part to another with no memory of what had just occurred. Even as an adult in her late thirties, she talked like a child.

Her therapy went on for eighteen consecutive years, and

then sporadically with large gaps, until the present, forty years later. Early on in therapy, the hardest part was keeping at least one adult-like part of her in the room. Later, she settled into four main parts (three four-year-olds and "Me," the adult). The early work involved helping her parts recognize current safety, the adult body, and the present time. We had to teach all the parts to know the year, the body's age, and what she was supposed to be doing at any minute.

Eventually we were able to do the trauma work by bringing parts, over and over again, to the safe present time, and letting them know that Me was in charge. We utilized EMDR, and many other techniques, through the years.

Now in her late seventies, Brenda has parts arising that came from her first days in the cult. She calls me, comes in, and we introduce the part to the safe present time, and the four established parts, and they hug her inside. Done! Until the next one shows up.

Good Sex

When I was in my twenties, I had a vivacious, very connected boyfriend. We mostly had amazing sex, except once in a while, right in the middle of things, he'd disappear. I asked him, "What happened? Where are you?" *I'm thinking about that guy who messed with me when I was twelve.* "Then stop right now and get here." He told me about the guy. He then oriented to his room and his adult bed. And I asked him, "Did that guy have these breasts?" *No.* "Did he have one of these?" (Pointing down.) *Absolutely not.* About five minutes later, he got completely oriented, and we picked up where we had left off. I asked him to tell me whenever that guy was in the room, so that we could always stop. After about three more times, the flash-backs stopped.

Later, when I started doing therapy with survivors of sex abuse, I remembered this. I taught people to say "Stop!" to get absolutely present, and to always ask for what they need to stay present, feel safe, and have a good time.

Finally

Sex abuse is devastating to experience and can profoundly affect sexual functioning until the traumas are resolved. Good therapy offers elimination of the flashbacks, current discomforts, dissociation, and avoidance that often accompany abuse histories. If you have this history, or any trauma history, I hope you find a good therapist with good therapies to clear all the trauma and bring in all the skills you need to connect, attach, stay present in your good current life, and have a great time.

References

Barbach, L. G. 2002. For Yourself: The Fulfillment of Female Sexuality. New York: Anchor Books.

De Jongh, A., and S. Matthijssen. 2020. EMDR 2.0: An Enhanced Version of EMDR Therapy. EMDR International Association. Accessed November 11, 2023. https://www.emdria.org/

National Center for Victims of Crime. 2023. "Child Sexual Abuse Statistics." Accessed October 28, 2023. https://victimsofcrime.org/child-sexual-abuse-statistics/.

National Sexual Violence Resource Center. 2023. "NSVRC Blogs." Accessed November 11, 2023. https://www.nsvrc.org/blogs/online-communities-survivors-websites-and-resources-offering-support-and-help.

OMGYES. 2023. "The Science of Women's Intimacy." Accessed October 28, 2023. https://go.omgyes.com.

Part Two

Intergenerational, Intersectional, and Culturally Embedded Trauma

Chapter 5

Black and African American Trauma Resilience in Flight

From Subservience to Liberation and the Stories in Between

Leann R. Johnson, MS

Geese—even geese—tire, moving, flying through their natural environment. Geese are built to fly, but no creature can do so without rest, even if they are doing what they are intended to do: fly. Imagine then if one must fly through that which is unnatural with barriers both known and unknown, thrown at you without warning. Would the geese not tire sooner, weaken? Perhaps grow ill? Perhaps drop to the ground with no hope of resuscitation?

One day in 2016, I was driving to work from my home in Vancouver, Washington, to Portland, Oregon. Weeks prior, my employer had promoted me to the interim role of director of the agency's equity and inclusion work. My dear, wise, and caring director had resigned, and I was to temporarily take her place. She had always likened our work, and our team, powering through the resistance of advancing health equity in a system steeped in the legacy of racial oppression, to geese, saying that when one of us tires another must move to the front to lead the way.

That morning, as I drove across the Interstate Bridge over

the Columbia River, approaching the Columbia Slough, I witnessed what I had often witnessed at that point of my journey. Geese. Hundreds of them flying in formation, beautiful, doing what their natural state intends for them. This time, however, was different. To my alarm, I saw something I had never seen before. The geese appeared to be in chaos. They were moving into formation then suddenly they were not. I was witnessing while superimposing what I was feeling: uncertainty, chaos, and fear that the employees entrusted to my leadership would suffer the same fate as those geese. My first thought was *they are in trouble*. I gasped. My breathing became shallow. I was afraid for them, not understanding that the geese knew what they were doing while actually fearing that I, on the other hand, may not.

What I do know is that the geese analogy remained true for me in what were to be rough and chaotic times ahead. I was the goose chosen to lead and chosen to do so because of my skills to navigate through chaos. The chaos was the reality of racism, and I was the person chosen to move through this very unnatural environment of racism, colonization, dehumanization, and harassment while working to instill policies and practices of justice and equity in a government system. The hazards of the job were like someone throwing stones or even a boulder heaved by a petard of hatred, designed to destabilize, and perpetuate the lie of white supremacy into our flock of geese. I was already tired. I was living with racial trauma and there was to be more where that came from in the coming weeks, months, and years.

A concept inspired by a 2005 commencement speech delivered by author David Foster Wallace at Kenyon College states that we often will not perceive the water in which we swim if all we have known is that space and place. One may comprehend that something is sustaining them, but one may not comprehend it as anything but "normal." This analogy can be adapted and said about the air in which one flies or moves in daily.

The air in which I fly does not seem "normal." It is the air in which most, if not all, people of color, women of color, and, more specific to my situation, Black women fly. It contains the toxicity of racism that comes in forms ranging from implicit to explicit, including bias, discrimination, a persistent narrative of dehumanization, damaging stereotypes, and so forth (DeGruy 2005). None of these ills of society, pollutants of the air, can be ignored. They consist of the dynamics and expectations set forth in our relationships perpetrated by 531 years of colonization of these lands that are the "United" States of America, the colonization and genocide of the original peoples of these lands, and the further colonization abroad which included the capture and enslavement of millions of African people—people stolen from their land (DeGruy 2005).

Going back to the original analogy, we must come to realize it is not so much the air that is the trouble. It is the pollutants that contaminate all our lives and well-being, our health, and our relationships. If air is what we need to survive and thrive, then it is the pollutants that choke us; choke us so we can no longer breathe deep for fear of taking in more that kills us, restricting the intake of the very oxygen that sustains our lives. In avoiding the pollutants, we diminish the very life-giving force that sustains us. Our own bodies rebel—our physical and mental health rebels— to protect our health and integrity. The colonial pollutants that society produces that we let in and settle in our bodies, are not unlike trauma. For people of color, the air and its toxicity can become one and the same.

Between that day in 2016 and today, I learned more about the pollutants than I ever wanted to know or experience. Those years, however, did not exist in isolation, as our relationships today among people, among women, among Black and white women do not exist free from our history—our history of racism in this country. This is what we fly in, and at times we do not even know. Until we know, accept, and redress the far-reaching damage that our racist history of genocide and enslavement has perpetrated (DeGruy 2005), until we mend and heal, until we understand how it affects you and me on a daily basis, we will be forced to navigate these hazards, these cultural land mines of the past, that remain ever present and real today. In the case of racial trauma, the core of healing relates to identity develop-ment, and forming one that breaks free of the shame of the racist narrative of inferiority, subservience, and dehumaniza-tion (Burke and Brown 2021).

This has been my journey.

When the Air Got Toxic and Breathing Became Shallow

When I was ten years old, my family moved from Portland, Oregon, to Vancouver, Washington. It was the summer of 1972, August. I remember being excited. I heard from my mom and dad that there were kids in the neighborhood, many around the same ages as me and my two sisters, Julie and Jenna. Julie, who was seventeen months younger than me, had just turned nine, and Jenna, the baby, was two. It all seemed wonderful and for a fleeting time, it was.

When we moved to our single-level ranch home in suburbia on Lupin Way, we were soon delighted to learn that there were not just kids, but literally at least one kid, if not more, in every household up and down Lupin Way and down a good portion of Dogwood Drive. The kids did indeed range from the ages of about eighteen months to fourteen years. All was as my parents had promised and exceeded our wildest dreams.

The 1972 school year started later that month. We got to go real school shopping, not for Catholic school uniforms but for "real clothes." At the time, I had not realized I would miss and long for that annual late-summer trip to Dennis Uniform, so much so that I later subjected my own children to the "horrors of Catholic school" and the wonders of the uniform store under the bridge in Portland. In actuality, my real horrors were yet to begin. Arriving at Benjamin Franklin Elementary School in Vancouver, Washington, that warm end-of-summer day, I was more excited than fearful for that moment. The moment was surely monumental not only for me but for Ben Franklin Elementary, as my sister Julie and I were likely the first Black children to walk in the doors of that school. I remember the exciting, free, and liberating feeling to this day, the smell of the lunch cafeteria (school lunch every day!), the classrooms that opened to the outdoors, and bathrooms shared between two classrooms where a child could just get up and go. There would be no group trips to the restroom down the hall, no hall pass, and no nun to convince that I really needed that hall pass even though the group trip had occurred in the last thirty minutes when I did not have to "go." The experience seemed liberating and free. Here I would finally fly away from the confines and constrictions of Catholic school and all the things in my life that seemed to want to push and punch me down. The latter was not consciously known, but I felt it. I *felt* it somehow every day of my life.

I do not recall the first time I heard it. The first time I heard the "n-word." It might have been when one child asked another child to do something, and the response was, "I'm not your n-word." It might have been when one child asked another, "Hey, where did you get your shoes?" and another answered, "Off a dead n-word." It might have been when a child yelled as I was playing in the school yard at recess, "That there is a black-face n-word." What I do remember is that the teacher never intervened, never put a stop to the language (that would not happen for another four years). I do remember that over time I could not control my neck as the stress embedded in my body and my head would start to shake and "bobble" beyond my control. I remember how I despised the study unit about the Civil War and the images in our textbook of all the Black people stacked up in the hull of a ship. I also remember that I grew physically weak and ill, and that I never told my parents.

There was also this thing. This thing with my breathing—the rapid succession of taking in air. My body, trying to breathe, trying to survive what in retrospect I know was deep, life-altering trauma. I was ten years old, and I was struggling with each racist event and, more tragically, each anticipated racist event. My body would brace and prepare, every day, for what was destined to come. This was my life. This seemed my fate. Breathing became a shallow, unnatural proposition.

Physical and Mental Health Harm

In retrospect, I have reflected on the harm, the disruption, the reset of the trajectory. Ten-year-olds! Ten-year-olds unwittingly perpetuated this country's legacy of racism and oppression, delivering the dehumanizing narrative of inferiority—my inferiority. Ten-year-olds absorbing and sending messages from parents, from the media, from the educational system, becoming agents in the perpetuation of intergenerational transmission of racism (DeGruy 2005). My trajectory, my childhood, was interrupted, and for decades to follow I would feel what I thought I was seeing in the chaos of the geese that day in 2016. I felt confused. I could not focus. I had slipped into undiagnosed depression and traumatic stress. My mom took me to the pediatrician, who did blood tests and found nothing wrong. Something was desperately wrong.

At the time, I had no words or way to make sense of what was happening to me or why, except to think that something was desperately wrong with me, not the rest of society. It was not until years later that I began to make sense of the ills of racism in our society and understand that racism served as a wicked seed responsible for ills in our mental and physical health as Black people.

In 2019 Columbia University released a report, "Addressing Mental Health in the Black Community," concluding:

Historically, the Black community was and continues to be disadvantaged in mental health through subjection to trauma from enslavement, oppression, colonialism, racism, and segregation. (Vance 2019)

In addition to mental health harm, there is a myriad of other ways Black people are physically harmed by trauma. For example, research from the Kaiser Family Foundation shows that a baby born to a Black person is more likely to die in their first year than a baby born to a white person—further underscoring the burden of racism, discrimination, and toxic stress. This remains true even when controlling for income and education, indicating that outcomes of this nature are rooted not in deficits related to the individual or even the community itself, but deficits in society, namely the long-standing burden of social injustice. (Latoya, Artiga and Ranji 2022).

Recalling the birthing experiences of two children, my situation does not fall far from these data points. The harm done by people entrusted with our care can have long-lasting implications, with harm running deeper because "helping professionals" were the perpetrators. When my second child was born, the nurse who was "caring" for us told me, "Your baby doesn't look Black. You're so lucky." As harmful as that comment was, steeped in a dehumanizing message of the inferiority of Black people (Walker 2020), it did not compare to my first birthing experience, where I suffered a postpartum hemorrhage, was slipping in and out of consciousness, and could get no traction of belief or action as I pleaded with the "helping professionals" entrusted with my care. Although this was 1991, today related stories have been told by Serena Williams, an internationally renowned athlete and Black woman (Walker 2020). What I heard from those "helping professionals" was, "Honey, childbirth is hard," as I was bleeding out. I am convinced that up until the moment that another OB-GYN came into the room and saw only a patient in distress, I was viewed through the lens of every stereotype that this room of predominantly white women was able to conjure.

I tell this story not only as prologue, but as a fiber in the fabric of trauma that in isolation may seem insignificant, yet in historical context is a more profound revelation. Harkening to the story in the school yard twenty years prior, something else happened the day the kid called me a "black-face n-word." Though I do not recall the exact progression of events, I do recall that there was another girl present. She was a little blond-haired girl with sparkly blue eyes, in the vicinity of the event. I place no blame on this little blond-haired girl yet recall that on that same day there was a call out of her humanity as well, which was quite the contrary to mine. The words from that kid turning his attention to the blonde-haired girl and looking back at me to be sure I heard the message were something like, "Now she, she is a good girl." He did not need to call me "bad girl" for me to know what he meant and why he meant it. (Once again, this was our nation's legacy of racism and oppression transmitted by a child!) I remember the words from that day, how they stung and demeaned me, and how they would continue to inform how I thought people regarded me and how I would implicitly regard myself.

Though I identify as a Black woman, my DNA tells a bit different and interesting story that includes white and Filipina heritage. On my mother's side of the family, I come from a long line of "light-skinned Black people," and from my father, a Black grandfather and Polish Austrian grandmother. In the dichotomous binary of either/or thinking, I defied description. The question "What are you?" or "Why are you so white?" or "Why are you so dark?" would render me immobile. It would create chaos in my head and body. My brain would stall out. Initially I would try to answer the question, yet my answer to them was rarely satisfactory.

When *mixed* hit the U.S. English vernacular, typically meaning half Black and half white, I embraced that term for a brief time until my mid-adult years and still had to field questions like, "Which one of your parents is white?" or "Which one of your parents is Black?" Once again, my answer of "neither" or "both" only rendered confusion. So in part to simplify, in part to embrace, and in part to understand the historical context of this nation and who I have always been to this nation, I changed how I labeled and regarded myself. I once heard a friend who is Black with some white heritage say, "We don't get pulled over because we are mixed," and that became enough for me to embrace a word and identity that I had long rejected in my childhood, as a teen, and in my years as a younger adult. This became my first act of liberation, unconscious at the time, yet, in retrospect, truly how I came to proudly refer to myself. In moments of reckoning around my identity, which is indeed a lifelong process, not simply a moment, the chaos quieted, and I could find my people, my worth, my formation, and my belonging. It was also the time I start to lose white "friends" and colleagues, white women, in particular.

The Virtue of White Women and Expectations of Subservience

Subservience is the willingness to obey others without questioning. The condition of being less important than something else or someone else. Synonyms include obedience, acquiescence, deference, reverence, docility, meekness, submission (Merriam-Webster n.d.). History has extolled the virtues of white women for centuries. The image of Manifest Destiny was anthropomorphized as that of a white, blonde woman in the 1872 painting *American Progress* by John Gast, depicting a larger-than-life figure of a white woman floating above people traveling to the western territories. The racist 1915 film *The Birth of a Nation* perpetuated the falsehood that Black people were "sex-crazed" and a threat to white women.

Between 1877 and 1950, there were 4,084 documented "racial terror lynchings" in the U.S., with 25 percent of lynchings of Black men related to what white mobs deemed to be criminal advances by Black men toward white women. Yes, the narrative of the virtuous, "good girl" white woman prevailed. This was further complicated and perpetuated examples of white women making false allegations against Black men (Equal Justice Initiative 2017). It was nothing short of terror and dehumanization that has insidiously morphed into a form of modern-day psychological enslavement. We must understand that violent terrorist acts by white people against Black people were designed specifically to maintain "racial hierarchy" and white supremacy (Equal Justice Initiative 2017). We must collectively acknowledge this to combat the harm and begin to heal the trauma that has attached to our modern-day relationships and interactions.

Dr. Isha McKenzie-Mavinga cites the dynamic of harm that originated in our relationships centuries ago, but remains present in modern-day interactions, as intergenerational transmission of ancestral baggage. Ancestral baggage is the culmination of past influences and trauma that clutch and harm not only current generations and current lives of Black people, but also the collective psyche. Subservience is one of the dynamics within ancestral baggage. We packed those bags centuries ago through power-ridden relationships that existed between people in previous generations. The failure to recognize and unpack this dynamic today creates complications for Black women in terms of our identities and our relationships with white women. Historical roots make for contemporary implications (McKenzie-Mavinga 2009). The expectation of subservience, however unconscious, is a modern-day remnant of the historical "racial hierarchy."

Historically, Black women were enslaved, deemed servants, mammies, the help, domestics, and so forth. All these roles or descriptors are positions of subservience, where the Black woman was "of service" to the head mistress of the house. While many of us would never intentionally want to perpetuate the dynamics of power over another person, we do, and we most likely do so unconsciously, fueled by the insidious nature of racism. The intergenerational transmission of racism— meaning the messages and stereotypes—are passed along, often unwittingly, from one generation to the next (DeGruy 2015; McKenzie-Mavinga 2009). According to Dr. McKenzie-Mavinga, transmission and related dynamics are what infect the collective psyche. Dr. Joy DeGruy Leary, author of *Post*

Traumatic Slave Syndrome, states that because we are often in denial about the existence and role of racism and enslavement, we have never truly had an intervention in the United States and, therefore, we, as a people, have never healed. (DeGruy-Leary 2005). For this reason, according to Dr. McKenzie-Mavinga, we remain at the mercy of the "destructive impulses" of the roles of oppressor and victim. Societal conditions and the dehumanizing narrative will continue to define the conditions of our relationships and roles, generation after generation, until there is an intervention. These roles manifest in our lives today and are particularly present in places where we convene and interact, including churches, schools, civic clubs, youth sports clubs, public transportation, and one of the greatest culprits of all, the workplace (DeGruy 2005; McKenzie-Mavinga 2009).

Breaking the Shackles

After graduating from university in 1984, I entered the nonprofit world of community activism. I had amazing people, mostly women, who lifted me up. While it helped my development and success, I realized in later years that this was a time in my life when I was "safe." My psyche was protected because I was, first, a young woman, so there was already an age-related power differential between me and my older mentors. I was appropriately respectful to my elders. I was in my place as a mentee and per my identity at the time, but it was not as much that I identified as "mixed," it was that I did not identify as "Black." Fact of the matter is that my worth, humanity, and positionality was conditional and paralleled the historical dynamic: The Black woman enslaved by the house could never rise above the house mistress and the subordinate could never question the master. The relationship and the well-being of that relationship (not the Black woman herself) was dependent upon the subservience of that Black woman, undermining her well-being and sense of worth (Johnson and McClure 2022).

It was not until two incidents with a work colleague that I headed toward the realization that I was living out, victimized by, and worse yet, perpetuating a role of subservience. Early on in my time with my current employer, I had a colleague who was lateral to me in the power structure. I did not report or answer to her. Yet not once but twice she called me out, first saying that "I needed to step up my game," erroneously assigning me fault in a situation, and a second time, calling me into her office and telling me that I was "on my high horse again." While in the moment we talked it through, again my brain stalled out and my body went into chaos.

For days, I carried each of those events. I could not shake off the pain, the trauma, and my go-to as an adult professional: sobbing uncontrollably in the bathtub. About a week after the second event, I heard myself ask aloud, "Why, Leann, why do you always overreact to these things?!" Shortly thereafter I wondered, "Why am I blaming myself for this?" Another phase of my liberation had begun as I worked to embrace the belief that I was worthy and, more importantly, I was not to blame. The conflict was bigger than me and it was even bigger than my colleague. What was unraveling between us was not just between the two of us, it was a matter steeped in our ancestral baggage, with all the complexities of power, expectations of subservience, and "stereotypes pervading both the Eurocentric black psyche and the Eurocentric white psyche" (McKenzie-Mavinga 2009, 97). Eurocentric dominance had been unconsciously adopted by Black and white people alike, insidiously steeped in historical legacy and trauma, and it was playing out in my workplace in real time.

From that point in time, the navigation became more fraught. While racism can hunt us down, denial can be superficial and attracts that which is superficial: superficial friends, superficial success, superficial well-being. As I sought the superficial to potentially avoid the pain of the trauma, it festered deeply within my body and my psyche. With each incident that I suppressed, I enabled the circumstances for the collective racist dynamics in our relationships and our systems to thrive. Not at all unlike Stockholm syndrome, we run the risk of over-identifying with our oppressor in the aptly named racial Stockholm syndrome theorized in 1993 (Huddleston-Mattai and Mattai 1993). This construct explores our relationship to internalized oppression, where we as people harmed by racism begin to believe the narrative that perpetuates it and seek assimilation to mitigate the harm (Walker 2020). This attempted assimilation only further undermines our wellness, physical and mental, and further punctuates the will of oppressive and racist systems. In other words, there are no shortcuts in reconciling and moving through the scourge of trauma, and racial trauma does indeed call for identity development, which reconciles shame that has been steeped in a racist narrative and fallacy of inferiority and dehumanization (Burke and Brown 2021).

The stronger my racial identity evolved, and the more I found resolution around that identity, white women who I thought were my friends, white colleagues who I thought respected me, and white supervisors who I thought supported me started "acting up." I pushed back on their assumptions around race and racism. I questioned actions and comments. I added information to provide another point of view. I stopped appeasing my oppressor. I was no longer going to be subservient. I soon discovered how many of my relationships were indeed based upon my, unconscious at the time, willingness to act in a historically defined role (McKenzie-Mavinga 2005). While I had been a racial justice activist in career and community settings, I was not necessarily an activist for my own well-being. I am evolving to become relentless in my pursuit of my own liberation from the unconscious subservience that was imposed and became part of my conditioning.

Another Pivotal Turn

The complexities of all that factors into trauma as it relates to an entire system that in essence conspires against your humanity and existence are beyond the confines of a single chapter or even book. To make these complexities easier to digest, I present stories that are the demonstration, the revelation, and the opportunity to heal all at once. Making sense of my surroundings in time, space, and place grounds concepts in story and metaphor. In 2022, I visited the National Museum of African American History and Culture in Washington, D.C., where several quotes by author and feminist activist bell hooks were displayed, citing better than I ever could:

"People resist by naming their history."
"Oppressed people resist by defining their reality."
"People resist by telling their story."

In the spirit of these bell hooks revelations, it was not until I co-conceived, co-wrote, and co-performed a two-woman experimental play called *Black Woman/White Woman* that my life, my plight, my worth, my healing, and my liberation came into fuller focus. What had been on the horizon of my life and what, at some level, I trusted was there came to be in the journey of creating "Black Woman." Throughout the play, I, as Black Woman, manipulate chains representing the ebb and flow of my journey of shackling and liberation. The chains at times are wrapped around my neck, wrapped around my wrists, loosened, tightened, and at one point totally released, falling in a clanking heap to the ground.

On November 4, 2008, a pivotal moment occurred in my life. I was in front of my television, awaiting the results of the election of the forty-fourth president of the United States. My experience in this country and cynicism related to racism told me it would never happen, that the U.S. would not in 2008 ever elect a Black man to the presidency of this country. But we did. Reflecting on where we are today in this country, it still seems nothing more than a fluke of a moment when we in this country were convinced or at least set to prove "we are not racist." No matter the reason, I took the moment and the eight years that followed as a bit of a reprieve.

The rest of the nation did as well, as rumors of a post-racial society emerged, and the U.S. went about its business as if the work of overcoming racism were complete. I recall speaking to a group of college students in a career development class about discrimination in the workplace as I had done the two previous years. I was all but shouted down by that class, criticizing me for perpetuating an old worn-out narrative that was of my generation, not theirs. The fact that they felt at liberty to do that and that there was no intervention by the instructor proved my point that we were not post-racial. The utter disrespect of a Black woman that they showed me, a professional in my field, showed ignorance about even very recent history and their naiveté. They treated me with the expectation that I would be subservient to their beliefs, and what I could do was respect-fully disagree and then eight or nine years later do a proverbial told-you-so with a smirk on my face. I would have liked to have been wrong, and my experience told me I was not. Even though it threw me, and I felt old familiar feelings arising, I was able to manage that situation (and what would have been emotional fallout and bathtub sobbing) with a new sense of fortitude. It was a fortitude that allowed me to regard the air, the pollutants, and still do what I was intended to do: fly. Dr. Rheeda Walker refers to this strength necessary to navigate, survive, and ultimately thrive in racist, non-liberated spaces as psychological fortitude, or PF (Walker 2020). If spaces cannot change or we cannot change them, we must find the strength we need to foster resilience and our own well-being. For me that is about perspective.

Harkening back to that historic election day in 2008, I remembered the growing disbelief as state after state got called for Barack Obama until finally later that evening, Barack Obama, senator from Illinois, was the projected winner of the race for president of the United States. Barack Obama, president-elect, would indeed be the forty-fourth president of our country and, in that moment, it felt like our country, like my country too. I do not remember all the details of the evening except running into, of all places, the bathroom. I looked in the mirror. Tears were running down my cheeks and I remember involuntarily drawing in a deep, deep breath. I shuddered. I had a sense of joy and belonging. In that breath, the truth of the moment crept in, and I smiled, shook my head in disbelief, and laughed. The reaction was not even so much around the fact that the U.S. would now have a Black president. It was that the U.S. would have a Black First Lady. Yes, we would have a Black First Lady and I could finally be the "good girl." The shackles released, clanking into a heap on the ground. This represented the release of shame, a dynamic that I had never explicitly considered part of my mental health landscape until reading *You Are Your Best Thing* (Burke and Brown 2021).

One might think that I, a sixty-one-year-old with all my life experiences of overcoming adversity and an MS in psychology, would not require such an affirmation of my worth and humanity. I, too, was surprised by my feelings of worthiness and liberation, yet my first instinct in the realization of this shame was to actually retreat to my shame. How could I not know? Why was I acting like a child, needing this type of external assurance that I was worthy? And there you have it: acting like a child. Shame settled into my body and psyche when I was ten years old. It settled in when I was a child in that schoolyard and was reinforced over and over again with each racist incident in my life. What followed as a young adult was my social justice activism, working to change the society that harmed me and that harms us. I had many successes in this realm: the white man who on my last day at one of my jobs came into my office to say goodbye and let me know I changed his outlook for the positive on race, or the headline and editorial in our local newspaper that said Clark County would not have known it had a problem with racism if not for my work in the community. My activism was vast and impactful, yet there I was with each "victory," withering on the vine, until for the first time in my life I recognized the shame that had burdened me. I named it, and recentered myself, once more, in my relentless pursuit to be my own activist by healing the shame.

In the Company of Birds

I wish I could have added to the sentence about the release of my shackles in 2008 "never to be retrieved or even regarded again," but that would be untruthful. The issue with racism as a source of trauma is that the acts have not gone away, nor have the racist structures currently embedded in the system. This dynamic is called PTSE, or persistent traumatic stress environments, a phrase illustrating the truth that this is not about us. We have not caused our trauma. The system, its structures, and its agents impose that trauma upon us (Burke and Brown 2022). We are not yet post-racial, as evidenced in part by the fact that hate crimes are on the rise (Novotney 2023). Some politicians are using the system to undermine and draw back civil rights, rather than protect or expand them. The racial justice reckoning following the murder of George Floyd in 2020 has, from my perspective, stalled. Even I, after all my work, can still, at times, fall prey to shackles and expectations of subservience (McKenzie-Mavinga 2009).

Through therapy and forms of artistic expression, including telling and owning my story and my reality, I am learning to make racism and its trauma matter less and less in my life. Racism, as Toni Morrison said, is designed to distract: "The function, the very serious function of racism is distraction. It keeps you from doing your work. It keeps you explaining, over and over again, your reason for being" (Forna 2022). Racism is designed to harm, and it does. The harm is real, and I must believe there is hope to overcome it. Fixing it means our white colleagues need to change, overcoming it means I need to find the psychological fortitude (Walker 2020) to overcome its effects. It does not and cannot mean I deny the existence of racism and the impacts of its trauma, but it does mean that I make it matter less so I can find my own sense of well-being and reinforce my resilience. To do otherwise is to put my stock in the oppressor, which means I am then relying upon my oppressor in some sort of absurd racial Stockholm syndrome relationship (Huddleston-Mataii and Mataii 1993), and I am much, much better than that.

When geese fly, they never rely on the strength of one to carry the flock. The lead goose rotates. Each goose takes their turn to let another rest. They make their way in a system that supports all. For a brief time in 2020, through the racial justice reckoning, we held glimmers of that hope and promise, just as we had done in 2008. Those of us who have carried the burden and lived the harm cannot wait for the system and people to change to find our own sense of liberation. My healing is contingent upon finding liberation in unliberated space, as I must interact with those spaces daily. When it is my turn to lead, I must lead, and when it is my turn to rest, I must rest. There is comfort and healing in knowing I am not alone and, more importantly, that I am not delusional, as some aspects of our society would have us believe. It is interesting that there is a new push to deem racism the delusion, meaning that if one believes that one people are inferior to another, that is mental illness (Walker 2020). I cannot help but wonder and speculate on the trauma that may have occurred in a racist's life that would make them, well, a racist.

Reflecting upon the women I have lost in my life—a friend, a colleague, a boss—I understand that white women have been traumatized in their lives and they too have a conspiracy against them. In the play *Black Woman/White Woman*, White Woman pursues understanding and humility as relentlessly as Black Woman pursues justice and healing. Most telling in the narrative of White Woman is:

As white women, our job is NOT to feel sorry for, not to "save" and not even to feel guilty about ... and definitely not to fear loss of power ... not to believe the lie. It is to see systemic issues, expose ourselves to, listen to, and believe the stories we hear, acknowledge, apologize ... see our own pain and contributions to the lie ... and **do our work to HEAL ourselves**. And do what we can from wherever we are to disrupt or create new healing systems ... [and] destroy the lie (Johnson and McClure 2022).

There is comfort and healing in knowing that I do not need to continue to play the role set for Black women from the play-book of history, and that I will not wait for the space to be granted or for someone else to unlock the shackles. The racial justice reckoning must be done on the terms of the people who are harmed, not the terms of the oppressor, who still may want to hold on to the keys and be an arbiter of power. It is true that, to a certain degree, my ability to heal is contingent upon the healing of my captor, yet I must demand that my own liberation happen on my terms and not theirs. This remains for me a tenuous proposition at best. The reflection or revelation is this: I live in a racist society. I, as a Black woman, am one of multiple targets of that racism. Many people in this country believe either implicitly or explicitly the narrative of inferiority of Black people (Walker 2020). But my stance is this: the racism that is enacted upon me does not define me.

Epilogue

The geese organize and reorganize as necessary for their health, well-being, and ability to support the greater good of their survival and ability to thrive. I only hope that we, as humans in this nation, can see that there is both a journey and a destination, and we will need to rely on each other to get there together. Do your work, and I will do mine. Find your people. Find your friends, even if they're not the kind of people you've usually hung out with in the past. Find your flock. We are not intended to go at life alone, and now more than ever, we need each other.

References

Novotney, A. 2023. "Hate Crimes Are on the Rise in the US. What Are the Psychological Effects?" American Psychological Association. www.apa.org/topics/gun-violence-crime/hate-crimes.

Burke, T., and B. Brown. 2021. *You Are Your Best Thing: Vulnerability, Shame, Resilience and the Black Experience, An Anthology*. New York: Random House.

Forna, A. 2022. "Racism as Distraction: Aminatta Forna Writes about Toni Morrison." Georgetown Medical Humanities Institute. https://medicalhumanities.georgetown.edu/media-and-scholarship/media/racism-as-distraction.

DeGruy Leary, J. 2005. Post *Traumatic Slave Syndrome: America's Legacy of Enduring Injury and Healing*. Uptone Press.

Equal Justice Initiative. 2017. *Lynching in America: Confronting the Legacy of Racial Terror*, 3rd edition. https://lynchinginamerica.eji.org/report.

Huddleston-Mattai, B. A., and P. R. Mattai. 1993. "The Sambo Mentality and the Stockholm Syndrome: Another Dimension to an Examination of the Plight of the African-American." *Journal of Black Studies* 23 (3).

Johnson, L., and K. McClure. 2022. *Black Woman/White Woman*. [play]

Hill, L., S. Artiga, and U. Ranji. 2022. "Racial Disparities in Maternal and Infant Health: Current Status and Efforts to Address Them." Kaiser Family Foundation. www.kff.org/racial-equity-and-health-policy/issue-brief/racial-disparities-in-maternal-and-infant-health-current-status-and-efforts-to-address-them.

McKenzie-Mavinga, I. 2009. *Black Issues in the Therapeutic Process*. New York: Bloomsbury.

Merriam-Webster. s/v "subservience." *Merriam-Webster Collegiate Dictionary*. www.merriam-webster.com/dictionary/subservience.

Walker, R. 2020. *The Unapologetic Guide to Black Mental Health: Navigate an Unequal System, Learn Tools for*

Emotional Wellness and Get the Help You Deserve. Oakland, CA: New Harbinger.

Vance, T. A. 2019. "Addressing Mental Health in the Black Community." Columbia University. www.columbiapsychiatry.org/news/addressing-mental-health-black-community.

Willoughby, Brian. 1997. "Challenging Bigotry, in Ourselves and Others." *Columbian* [*Vancouver*], January 19, 1997, B1.

Chapter 6

The Return Home

An Intersection of African American Intergenerational Trauma and Family Systems Theory

Javelin L. Hardy, LMSW

I returned home to continue childhood healing; the reality was the Creator removed me from an environment of family trauma, addiction, and family secrets.

In 2021, I had a heavy calling and longing to return home to Minden, Louisiana. I needed to obtain a family attorney to complete legal land successions and obtain ownership of the property my ancestors left me. I also longed for my father's love.

At the age of fifty-one, I packed up my life after living in Portland, Oregon, for thirty years. My children were shocked, but they knew I always wanted to return to Louisiana to retire. To my surprise, this place was no longer my home. In the words of my childhood friend Michael Munson, "Jay, Minden is our roots, and Portland is your new home." I grew up with a lot of strong African Americans who were entrepreneurs, heavily involved in the community, and a part of political arenas; many served as district councilmen/women. There are streets named after these ancestors along with abandoned homes on these same streets. These homes now need to be torn down because their spirits are no longer alive.

The value of ancestral land is not honored, and the dreams of my ancestors were taken to other cities and states. Looking at those houses, I felt like *time* stood still. The fragments of the crack cocaine drug area still have my people by the neck and ankles, and the remnants of alcohol has sucked souls to death. The dead spirits rise out of the earth, pulling them down, and they walk around looking like dead, hollow bodies.

I pay homage to my ancestors, the Musgrove, Cosby, Edward, Reeder, Anderson, Hardy, Hawkins, and Robinson families.

My grandfather Eugene Anderson, who was married to my grandmother Lula B. Anderson (my grandfather John Wesley Hardy's mother), left me his property. To my surprise, for me to totally inherit the property, he should have removed Lula's name from the property, so I had to pay for successions on all deceased ancestors. Lula B. Anderson, John Wesley Hardy, Vera Hardy, Rosemary Hardy, and Jeroldine Hardy. My siblings signed their part of the property over to me because they had no interest. I had to provide deeds, birth certificates, and death certificates to show proof of relationships and kinship. This was a very emotional process because I realized that the three men in my family—John Wesley Hardy, Leon Hardy, and Eugene Anderson—bought property together and helped each other pay off their property.

Learning all this and seeing the amount of property abandoned made me wonder: Did my generation understand what it took for our ancestors to inherit the land? I can only imagine the environmental trauma my ancestors faced. Environmental trauma is defined as emotional, physical, or psychological responses to an event, community environment, or series of events that has lasting adverse effects on an individual's functioning. Environmental trauma mostly describes natural disasters; here I am speaking from the traumatic experiences (discrimination) of not being able to purchase land as Black people, not being able to move to certain neighborhoods, not having adequate water, or plumbing, as well as lack of healthcare. Most of the people in my neighborhood were entrepreneurs or inventors and bargained services with each other to take care of the neighborhood. If it wasn't for Black churches and the Masonic Grand Lodge, there wouldn't have been any social services in the Black community.

I remember my grandfather sharing how my great-grandmother could have survived if the hospital in town provided medical care to "Black folks." People suffered not only from their medical traumas but also from trauma due to discrimination in medical systems. Because they did not receive medical care as "Black folks," they had a higher death rate for basic medical conditions that could have been treated. My ancestors had to drive thirty to forty-five minutes to get medical care because the hospital in town continued to deny care to African Americans. Their only alternative in town was to trust an unlicensed "medicine doctor" in the community, or find a white doctor that they could trust, and there were not that many of them.

After a year there, I decided to run for district councilwoman. I was asked why I wanted to run for office, and I told them I wanted to honor my ancestors and respect the land they left. As I campaigned in my area, I would ask neighbors what changes they would like to see, and most of them couldn't tell me anything except to lower their electric bill cost. These neighbors had multiple abandoned homes around them, no parks, and the grade school had been torn down, so the neighborhood by the school was now gone as well. I felt they were accustomed to poverty and abandonment, so I could under-stand why they couldn't see what I saw.

I felt myself getting depressed and second-guessing my decision to return home because, spiritually, I saw my side of town stuck with abandoned homes, churches, alcoholism, and addiction. I asked a lot of friends and loved ones who had moved away why they did. They shared that moving was their way out of poverty, racism, and dysfunctional family behaviors that continued now as a part of some of the black culture in Minden, Louisiana. They also asked me why I would ever move back here. For those who did return to visit, they wouldn't stay more than two to three days because, they shared, "It's a deadness there and it makes me feel sad."

I remember in 1990, I left this place on a Greyhound bus with my son and $200. The Journey home was to bring closure to my childhood trauma.

In my last book, *It Takes a Journey to Heal*, I revealed how one must be ready to heal to start the Journey (Hardy 2020). What was revealed on this Journey is that I had unhealed trauma from:

My relationship with my father
My relationship with childhood friends
Wanting to confront one of my childhood abusers
The blindness of addiction and Christianity
The trauma passed down to my sons

In 2010, I began the Master of Social Work program at Portland State University on a journey to understand my family and the behaviors and addictions that they had passed on to their descendants. I learned about family systems theory by Dr. Murray Bowen. Dr. Murray Bowen was an American psychiatrist and a professor of psychiatry who was among the pioneers of family therapy and noted founder of systemic ther-apy. Bowen suggested that "individuals cannot be understood in isolation from one another, but rather as a part of their family, as the family is an emotional unit" (Bowen 1976). This was my awakening moment because I learned my family didn't teach me how to deal or not deal with my emotions. I would have loved to witness healthy relationships and marriages as a young girl because I'm attracted "with the familiar" unconsciously. I'm familiar with abuse and domestic violence in the home, as well as drugs and alcohol.

As I look back on my family life, there were constant struggles with poverty, paying bills, domestic abuse, family disputes, and settling in unhealthy/abusive relationships.

At no time in this memoir am I disrespecting or putting down anyone in my family. I just feel there was a foundation laid by my grandmother that my mother could have capitalized on, but unfortunately drugs and unhealthy lifestyles took precedence over important life decisions. My grandmother owned the first African American kindergarten and Head Start school in Minden, Louisiana, and was a graduate of Grambling State University. My mother and my aunt Rosemary Hardy were both intelligent women. Unfortunately, they grew up during a time when drugs changed their lives and children were abandoned, which created kids not being protected and safe from seeing drug use and sexual abuse. I grew up as a latchkey kid, which made me become independent at a very young age. Latchkey kids learned how to cook, clean, wash laundry, take the bus, get ready for school, do our homework, and work at early ages because our parents had to work to provide.

In seeing the choices my mother, and a lot of parents in the eighties made, I, and people of my generation, went headlong into education, moving and dismantling generational behaviors by uprooting ourselves from our small town in Minden, Louisiana. My mother's father was an alcoholic, so I understand now why she married an alcoholic. My father and stepfather both served in Vietnam, and my father is an alcoholic. I also found out my father had post-traumatic stress disorder along with other mental health issues.

I've had my share of men who had some of the same characteristics as my father. So one day, I realized I became a runner who sabotages relationships with men who reminded me of my father or childhood. I also realized I "date the familiar" unconsciously because I was reared around these behaviors of alcohol and abuse. Dating the familiar unconsciously means I am attracted to men who carry the characteristics of my father: alpha men, alcoholics, and men who step out on their spouses— aka cheat. These are men who had multiple families and whose children met each other later on in life, in school or at funerals, causing more grief and pain. I discovered my unconscious behavior five years ago during counseling. I also discovered I have major anxiety in relationships with black men because, in my mind, some kind of abuse or addiction will show soon, which has caused me to self-sabotage relationships. I also ignore red flags until it's time to leave. My trauma response is fight-or-flight.

I use Bowenian family systems theory from an African American cultural perspective from the South that consists of religion, addiction, outside children, and adultery.

Triangulation

Bowen theory is formally made up of eight remarkably cohesive concepts that deal with the human family and with the individual. The first concept is *triangles*. The theory states that the triangle, a three-person emotional configuration, is the molecule or the basic building block of any emotional system, whether it is in the family or any other group. "The triangle is the smallest stable relationship system" (Bowen 1976).

Any time you try to better yourself and break off from the dysfunction of the family, you're seen as "stuck-up" or "bougie" by family or community members who spread rumors and gossip. There is a form of jealousy that causes tension within the family because the two people who keep up most of the drama traumatize the third person who's trying to break free from the family trauma and anxiety. This dynamic of hostility can also be directed toward those breaking free from churches, sororities, and fraternities, or any organization that forms cliques and elites where classism exists, which leaves poorer and uneducated Black folks in poverty and addiction.

Triangulation can also be seen when a couple who don't have a healthy relationship use their child to communicate when they don't get along. This dynamic causes the child to be caught in the middle of "adult issues," causing the child to have anxiety and "people-please," trying to get both parents to love them and put them first. Triangulation can cause the child to feel that they are the parents' trauma-dumping bucket, where the parents are sharing their trauma stories to the child and putting the other parent down. They try to have the child "choose" a parent by saying negative things and explaining adult issues that the child is too young to understand. These behaviors continue to make the child feel unheard, unseen, or unloved. My sons are now adults and have shared some of the things they experienced as children when I raised them, being overprotective, strict, and authoritarian. I know I projected my childhood fears onto my children, and in some ways this has caused them to experience anxiety. The emotion of anger was taught instead of how to regulate emotions.

Emotional Cutoff

The second concept is *cutoff*. An average family situation in our society today is one in which people maintain a "distant and formal relationship with the family of origin, returning home for duty visits at infrequent intervals" (Bowen 1976). Black folks I know who cut off their family left sexual abuse, family abuse/violence, trauma, and addiction. I cut off my mother for years when she struggled with addiction and remained in an abusive relationship. I wouldn't take my sons around my mother and stepfather. The separation, isolation, and withdrawal were detrimental for me but necessary for the protection of my children because I didn't want them to suffer from the abuse I endured as a child. I didn't want them to witness abuse and inherit anxiety and feeling unsafe as kids.

The post-traumatic stress disorder (PTSD) I endured as a child consisted of adults fighting verbally, physically, and emotionally while using drugs and alcohol. Some fights were caused by family members being unfaithful in relationships, some started from an altercation in a bar or club that was brought home, waking up the children in the middle of the night. These fights created tremendous anxiety and fear.

The definition of PTSD is a psychiatric disorder that may occur in people who experience or witness a traumatic event, series of events, or set of circumstances. People with PTSD experience intense, disturbing thoughts and feelings related to their experience that last long after the traumatic event has ended. They may relive the event through flashbacks or nightmares, they may feel detached or estranged from other people (American Psychological Association n.d.).

It's amazing how you're treated poorly when you don't want to drink, go to church, be a part of multiple relationships, cheat with people's wives or husbands, or have multiple children. In the words of brother Resmaa Menakem: "Unhealed trauma acts like a rock thrown into a pond; it causes ripples that move outward, affecting many other bodies over time. As it is passed on and gets compounded through other bodies in a household, it can become a family norm. And if it gets transmitted and compounded through multiple families and generations, it can start to look like culture" (Menakem 2017, 39).

It appears to be an honor and privilege to have multiple "baby mommies" or "baby daddies." The reality is these are broken homes of children crying out for the attention of their parents. This is also the new era of the "side piece," where someone is married or in a committed relationship but has another person on the side. Multiple triangulations and dysfunctional relationships are being created in these situations, and children are being born into this chaos.

This is "the culture, the trauma" that leaves innocent children abandoned and feeling alone. These are the behaviors that made me cut my family off, along with crack cocaine use and domestic abuse. Where there are drugs and abuse, there are incidents of trauma where children are not being protected.

Brother Resmaa describes how trauma can spread between bodies, like a contagious disease. He also explains how "someone with unhealed trauma chooses dirty pain over clean pain, the person may try to soothe his or her trauma by blowing it through another person—using violence, rage, coercion, deception, betrayal, or emotional abuse" (Menakem 2017, 40).

This dynamic is passed on unconsciously to the family, especially in small bodies. "Children are highly susceptible to being victimized by adult trauma and their nervous systems are overwhelmed by things that older, more experienced nervous systems can override. Just imagine how this depletes small bodies 'bandwidth' in learning, growing and maintaining healthy hygiene (e.g., trying to not wet the bed when adults fight or feeling like someone will come in the room and harm you with physical or sexual violence)" (Menakem 2017, 41).

My mother passed away in 2012, and my brother advised us we should have a relationship with our stepfather to honor our mother, since he was her husband. This man didn't bring anything positive into our home, and it took years for me to forgive him after my mother's passing. Being in a home as a child surrounded by drug use and domestic abuse always kept me on edge, being awakened at night due to fights and my body in the stage of "fight," because anytime my stepfather acted as if he was going to abuse my mother, we were going to protect her. So being asked by my brother to continue to check on him when my inner child was finally safe felt like asking me to go back in time to watch my mother get beaten.

The emotional cutoff helped my grieving process, because every time I saw him the suppressed memories in my mind and body would come alive and activate my central nervous system and make me relive my childhood; the safe thing for me was to "run and stay gone."

The return home expecting to reunite a relationship with my father was heartbreaking. Expecting to have my father in my life and discuss all the childhood issues, as well as not knowing how to relate and love a black man on an emotional level, was what I wanted to heal. I wanted to learn how to have a healthy relationship with my father, to work on my "daddy issues." The reality was my father was not mentally or emotionally available at the age of seventy-three. I've been waiting most of my life to gain wisdom and knowledge from my father, his failed mistakes, and things he learned. Instead, his ten-year-old inner child was still present and stronger than ever with a continuous addiction to alcohol, and his mental health needs had gone unaddressed and untreated.

I found myself moving no more than two miles away but

went half a year not even talking to my father due to keeping my inner child safe from the abusive child that he was. The inner child is described as "a person's supposed original or true self," especially when regarded as damaged or concealed by negative childhood experiences. I found out my father also grew up in a violent home of domestic abuse, his mother being in hospital due to mental abuse and being shot by her husband, made worse by living in poverty. My father was drafted and sent off to Vietnam and fought in the Vietnam War. I also learned my father left to go stay with his father as a child and that his father was an abusive alcoholic.

I learned that my father has complex trauma, which is prolonged or repetitive exposures to a series of traumatic events, within which individuals perceive little or no chance to escape. In complex trauma, the child's exposure to multiple traumatic events—often of an invasive, interpersonal nature—is wide-ranging, and it has long-term effects. These events are severe and pervasive, such as abuse or profound neglect (National Child Traumatic Stress Network n.d.).

Family Projection Process

The third concept in Bowenian family systems theory is the *family projection process*, through which parental undifferenti-ation (parents not establishing themselves as having different roles in the family than their children, and then projecting their issues onto their kids) impairs one or more children operating within the father-mother-child triangle. "It exists in all gradua-tions of intensity, from those in which impairment is minimal to those in which the child is seriously impaired for life, the process is so universal it is present to some degree in all fami-lies" (Bowen 1976, 65).

My siblings consist of an older brother and younger sister.

I'm a middle child. My mother allowed my brother to drink and smoke with her when he was growing up. His introduction to alcohol was at home. My baby sister was around my mother and stepfather when they were heavily using crack cocaine and drinking alcohol. My sister is in recovery from pills and alcohol. I inherited the behaviors of getting into unhealthy relationships and having children by men who didn't want to raise their children.

My children inherited abandonment and anxiety by not having their fathers in their lives. I didn't realize how much this affected them until they become teenagers. My oldest son developed a temper to deal with his loss of not having a father. My youngest son's father was physically in his life but was never there for him mentally or emotionally until he became a grown man. My sons are now thirty-three and thirty years of age and both are fathers themselves. They are emotionally and mentally available for their children and are doing a lot of "undoing" of passed on behaviors and addictions. Undoing is a defense mechanism in which someone tries to cancel out or revert an unhealthy or aggressive thought or action by engaging in opposite or contrary behavior (Costa 2020).

My brother suffered a heart attack five years ago, and congestive heart failure runs in the family. My grandfather died from a massive heart attack, and my mother as well. My brother continues to drink alcohol and has a pacemaker. My father continues to battle with alcohol addiction at age seventy-three. My mother's father, John Wesley Hardy, was an alcoholic, my deceased mother, and her husband as well.

My half-brother on my dad's side is incarcerated, and when he is in the community, he uses alcohol and synthetic drugs— "mojo" is what they call it. These substances cause you more anxiety, paranoia, and depressive symptoms than what's seen in natural cannabinoid users.

My siblings and I came from the same home and had three different fathers who had different backgrounds and trauma histories. My father was drafted during Vietnam, my brother's father died from a construction incident, and my sister's father died from cancer and liver disease.

We all made different decisions when it came to using alcohol and drugs. I was the little girl who knew what was coming next once someone drank or used drugs. At an early age, I learned there was a process to adults' actions when they did drugs, and someone was always abused or injured, which caused family trauma. In my case, sexual trauma and abandonment came from being in this environment. When a child's parents are intoxicated, they aren't safe for that child.

I would say that worry, anxiety, and depression were projected on me and my siblings as children. My mother worked two jobs on average with very low pay. I remember the family receiving government aid and WIC. My mom always worried about paying bills, buying school clothes, and having no more money than a month's expenses. As I raised my sons, I've always had multiple jobs and various hustles on the side. Even though I made more financially, I still stressed about bills even when I was able to pay them and had monies remaining. The lack of understanding from never being taught how to budget and save creates a mindset of poverty even when I was successfully working in a blue-collar field.

As I look back, I realize that I conceived my first child in a stressful environment and was also around cigarettes. Feeling like I let myself and family down, I know I shared anxiety and depression with my unborn son. Raising two sons, I always felt on-edge, stressed, tired, upset because I was left alone raising two young Black men, while healing from my own childhood trauma.

Multigenerational Transmission Process

The family projection process continues through multiple generations. In any nuclear family, there is one child who is the primary object of the family projection process. This child emerges with a lower level of differentiation than the parents and does less well in life. Other children, who are minimally involved with the parents, emerge with about the same levels of differentiation as the parents. Those who grow up relatively outside the family emotional process develop better levels of differentiation than the parents. If we follow the most impaired child through successive generations, we will see one line of descent producing lower and lower levels of differentiation. If we follow the line through the children who emerge with about the same levels of differentiation, we see a remarkable consistency of family functioning through the generations. If we follow the multigenerational lineage of those who emerge with higher levels of differentiation, we will see a line of highly functioning and very successful people (Bowen 1976, 66–67).

I found myself setting myself apart from my family when I had my sons. I attended college to learn and understand that the environment I was raised in was unhealthy. I don't have to continue to pass on these generational behaviors and traumas. I moved, left a culture that I knew if I didn't leave, I would pass on more trauma than I already possessed.

The Family Diagram

I grew up with family members who lived to be in their mid-eighties to mid-nineties, grew our own food, and paid for the homes they owned as well as the land. They were entrepreneurs and supported each other's businesses within the Black community. The health disparities are high blood pressure, diabetes, and cancer. My people were hard workers, dealt with racism, and didn't do well teaching my parents emotional processes in families. If I was to research our history, I would find that the men were torn away from the family during slavery, so they had to learn how to be husbands as well as fathers. After that, they were drafted into wars and returned home dealing with addiction and post-traumatic stress disorders. This is how the traumatized "emotional unit" developed, from slavery and war. So we are looking at generations of trauma. We're also looking at families being created by ancestors who never got emotional or mental help from slavery and war.

Sibling Position

My siblings consist of my older brother, younger sister, and three stepbrothers. I'm a middle child, and I had caretaker responsibilities as early as ten years old. I had to cook, iron my mom's uniforms, go to the laundromat by myself, and wash for a household of five. My older brother didn't have a lot of responsibilities, and my baby sister was not taught how to cook or do house duties. My stepbrothers didn't have any home duties as well. All four brothers struggled with alcoholism, and all except one have been incarcerated. My sister and I, unfortunately, are survivors of childhood sexual abuse. My sister struggled with addiction due to her childhood sexual abuse.

Societal Emotional Process

Bowen describes the triangle that exists in all relationships, and that was a small clue. When a family is subjected to chronic, sustained anxiety, the family begins to lose contact with its intellectually determined principles and to resort more and more to emotionally determined decisions to allay the anxiety of the moment. Bowen states we are in a period of increasing societal anxiety, and society responds to this with emotionally determined decisions. This results in more Band-Aid legislation, which increases the problems, and that cycle keeps repeating, just as the family goes through similar cycles to the state, what we call emotional illness. (Bowen 1976).

As I reflect on my family history and root cause of how the trauma began, I see that, unfortunately, it has become a "culture" passing on learned dysfunctional behaviors and addictions. Brother Resmaa Menakem argues, 'It's not a culture; it's a traumatic retention that has lost its context over time. So what did my family lose four generations before me? We were sold, separated, forced to be in wars, and drugs infiltrated into our communities. The "war on drugs" brought crack cocaine into our neighborhoods, wiped out many homes, and took our parents away. Our lives were lost, freedoms taken away, ethics, and values were lost. As Brother Menakem says, "Individual personality flaws, dysfunctional family dynamics, or twisted cultural norms are sometimes manifestations of historical trauma (Menakem 2017, 39).

There now exists research on how trauma can be inherited genetically, how it can change the expressions of the DNA in cells, and how these changes can be passed from parent to child. My mother had me when she was fifteen years old, and my father was being drafted to go serve in the Vietnam War. My mother never talked about her traumatic childhood, but when she passed, I spoke to a cousin who let me know my grandfather (John Wesley Hardy) would terrorize the family when he was intoxicated. I know my father was physically abused by his father for his entire childhood. So we have two adults who grew up with childhood trauma and produced a baby (me) who inherited their trauma through their DNA, which produced stress hormones in my mother's body, and affected the nervous system of my developing body in utero.

I can trace four generations back to where my family suffered from slavery, wars, and drugs. I can see how complex trauma has affected my entire family, especially my father. Complex trauma usually occurs as a result of repeated trauma experienced by a child or young person, although it can also occur as a result of repeated traumatic experiences as an adult. Some people experience trauma across their lifespan. My hope and prayer is that my family and I continue to work on our individual and collective healing. I hope you have learned something from an African American cultural perspective. If you are a counselor, social worker, or in the medical field, understand that we must "hear the story" of our clients to have empathy for them and leave them a safe space to speak their truth.

References

American Psychiatric Association. n.d. "Diagnostic and Statistical Manual of Mental Disorders (DSM-5-TR)." Accessed October 25, 2023. www.psychiatry.org/psychiatrists/practice/dsm.

Bowen, Murray. 1976. Quoted in Roberta M. Gilbert. 2004 and 2006. *The Eight Concepts of Bowen Theory: A New Way of Thinking about the Individual and the Group.* Virginia: Leading Systems.

Costa, Rui M. 2020. "Undoing (Defense Mechanism)." In *Encyclopedia of Personality and Individual Differences,* edited by Virgil Zeigler-Hill and Todd K. Shackelford, 5668–89. New York: Springer.

Hardy, Javelin. 2020. *It Takes a Journey to Heal.* Oregon: Dancing Moon.

Menakem, Resmaa. 2017. *My Grandmother's Hands: Racialized Trauma and the Pathway to Mending Our Hearts and Bodies.* Las Vegas: Central Recovery.

National Child Traumatic Stress Network. n.d. "About Child Trauma" Accessed October 25, 2023. www.nct-sn.org/what-is-child-trauma/about-child-trauma.

Chapter 7

How Feminism Saved My Life

Christine Forner, MSW, RSW

It has only been about forty years since sexual violence and domestic abuse have been seen as things that need our attention. Prior to this, rape, incest, and domestic abuse were not viewed as all that damaging, or that these were made-up events or exaggerations used to gain attention or revenge. Many of our laws that make these incidents illegal are less than forty years old. Even to this day, many acts of devastating coercive control are not deemed a criminal act, and those that are deemed unlawful are rarely prosecuted. Forty years is such a small drop in an 8,000-year-old bucket. The true amount of harm that is occurring from continual attempted genocide, not only of women but of people of color, and the still current issues of ownership of women and children, has yet to be fully comprehended.

Before the 1980s, violence against women was not part of any discussion within psychology, social work, or psychiatry. Even today, discussions on the truly damaging impact that misogyny and patriarchy have on every single person's health are not taking place. No real connection is drawn between misogyny and psychopathy, patriarchy and an entitlement to torture humans. The women's movement brought the realities of interpersonal harm out of the dark, but we still do not connect the dots of what misogyny is. Patriarchy will always be present if we do not get a full grip of the traumatic devastation that misogyny has wrought on all of humanity.

Misogyny is the original and continual attachment wound that becomes exponentially more damaging in a patriarchal world. Misogyny spawns psychopathy, sociopathy, and narcissism. Misogyny kills the most vital aspects of humanity: compassion, empathy, attunement, and connection. Feminism has brought these issues to the forefront, and feminism will hold us together.

In 1990, I had just finished a diploma in social welfare. I wanted to be a social worker, to help others, but my twenty-year-old self really had no idea what this meant. I had yet to be diagnosed with a writing disability, so I had little understanding as to why I was unable to achieve grades high enough to get into university to complete a bachelor's degree. I wanted to go to university full-time, so I decided to try to increase my grade point average in order to pursue a bachelor's in social work. At that time, you could take classes at the university on a part-time basis without having to qualify as a full-time student. I started to chip away by taking various courses that could apply toward an eventual degree. Most of the psychology classes were full, and you could not take any social work classes if you were not part of the designated program. However, there were plenty of women's studies and art history classes available. I was not all that interested in art history, so I took my first women's studies class. I had no idea that I was walking into a course that would influence my life more than any other class I would take, and that the trajectory of my life was about to be swiftly and dramatically altered. I had no idea that this first, single class in studying how women experience life would save me a thousand times over.

I continued to take two or three classes a semester for five years until I had enough classes for a full degree. I did eventually get my Bachelor of Arts and Master of Social Work degrees, but not until I had a foundational degree in women's studies. For me, these classes not only taught me an aspect of humanity that is not commonly known, but they taught me that there is so much more going on that we will never see or know if we are not aware that the patriarchy exists. Not a day goes by where I am not influenced by those first classes that were based in understanding the effects of misogyny and how the patriarchy influences all of us.

We have an enormous amount of information on the multitude of ways that we are all impacted by women not being treated as equal members of society. Data shows that the patriarchy manifests in all aspects of humanity. We have several theories as to why the patriarchy exists, which are related to some type of "normal" behavior that has somehow been exaggerated by some type of environmental influence, such as the theory that the patriarchy started because of the "uncivilized, but wholly understandable" need to protect and fight for one's hard-earned resources that came with the advent of agriculture and land ownership (Ananthaswamy and Douglas 2018). Or the theory that men are physically stronger, and it is the strength that helped us in the natural world. This theory states that men are the ones who are supposed to protect and defend women and children, and that men are inherently violent, aggressive creatures who need to fight for their alpha role and procreate to spread their DNA like other mammals do. Both theories excuse and normalize misogyny and patriarchy. To date, there is no theory that accurately articulates how damaging, aberrant, and cataclysmic of an event misogyny really was and is for our species and how the patriarchy is the antithesis of humanity—anti-human, if you will.

As much as we know about the how and what of misogyny and patriarchy, we still lack a theory as to why it exists in the first place. Every theory has an assumption, subtle or strong, that men are naturally aggressive, greedy, and selfish, and that it is only through reeducation or an enforced moral code that we can rid the world of this grossly assumed-to-be-biologically-normal, yet outdated, inequality.

Society does not acknowledge that for hundreds of thousands of years the imbalance of power between men and women, enforced through violence and trauma, did not exist. We do not have discussions that take what we know from the world of complex trauma, dissociation, attachment theory, and the polyvagal theory and apply these to misogyny and patriarchy. We need to have discourse that incorporates current scientific information that strongly contradicts assumed genetic power dynamics.

What we have learned in the last forty years or so is that misogyny and the patriarchy are abnormal and unnatural for humans. This information directly contradicts millennia-long enforced false beliefs. The most influential psychologists and psychiatrists in the realm of complex trauma, mental health, post-traumatic stress, dissociation, and attachment need to acknowledge how misogyny and the patriarchy profoundly injure all humans and often lie at the root of traumatizing behaviors, such as personal and systemic violence against women and girls, and anybody else who is "feminized" in our society. Based on what we know about trauma, misogyny and the patriarchy must be symptoms of a massive interpersonal injury that occurred a long time ago.

If we were to have these professional and societal conversations, it would become evident that misogyny has been as devastating to our species as the meteor that forever altered evolutionary trajectory was to the dinosaurs. It would become obvious that we humans must have gone through some type of catastrophic event that resulted in the hatred, fear, and 8,000-year-long attempted genocide, as well as the private torturous degradation, of those who are perceived as weak or vulnerable. It would be well known that there is no real evidence within our brain structures to support the narrative that males are like this because they inherently just are.

What is still missing from the conversation is viewing misogyny and patriarchy through a trauma lens. What is absent from the general dialogue is some basic commonsense thinking and seeing the fact that if men were "just like this"—violent, uncaring, stoic, distant, individual—then their behavior would not be as injurious as it is. Misogyny and patriarchy cannot be normal states of humanity because they are clearly created by being harmed, abused, or neglected as infants and children. If the trauma lens were used more broadly in discussions of patri-archy, the knowledge that when infants and children are cared for and tended to both physically and emotionally, with secure and supportive parents, misogyny and patriarchy do not exist, would be far more widespread.

We have known for at least forty years that childhood sexual abuse and neglect are childhood torture. What was strongly suspected since the 1970s has been unequivocally proven time and time again, from a wide range of academic and clinical sources. It is factual information that human infants cannot tolerate being ignored, hit, or sexually objectified in any way (Briggs et al. 2021). We know, beyond a shadow of a doubt, that humans cannot handle, in any way, human-to-human passive and active harm. This includes the odd response of disdaining anyone and anything that resembles what is cultur-ally considered female. Yet instead of saying, "wait a minute, this just can't be right," because there is no neurobiological, biomechanical, sensorimotor, affective, or other scientific evidence inside *Homo sapiens* that supports the theory that humans are primarily violent, the leading authorities in the world of trauma and attachment never discuss this glaringly obvious conundrum. Instead of taking in the information that humans are not innately violent, the largest contributors to the study of humanity continue to incorporate the narrative that accepts the myth that humans, especially male humans, are violent because of natural biology rather than cultural imperative born out of trauma wounding.

If we assume that misogyny is natural, instead of being the result of some type of species-altering injury that created patriarchy, we will never be motivated to comprehend how profoundly wounded we all are. If we continue to agree with the notion that humans are fundamentally violent and inherently psychopathic, we will never even begin to imagine what is normal for the human being. If we continue to see something that is truly messed up as normal, no matter how much we learn about what traumatization looks like from a behavioral and neurobiological perspective, we will never figure out how to stop psychopathy in all its iterations.

The notion that rape, sexual assault, domestic violence, coercive control, and greed are normal is absurd and flies in the face of what we know about Indigenous early humans. It is incredibly obvious that we should not be hurting each other, but this notion is not a common one. The Diagnostic and Statistical Manual and the International Classification of Disease discuss hundreds of ways that our mentality can and does go wrong, but nowhere in either book does the issue of sexual or physical abuse or neglect enter in as etiology. It is rather baffling, especially after 130 years of consistent scientific investigation starting with Pierre Janet, that continually shows how individually, socially, and economically devastating these injuries are, that still extraordinarily little is done to stop these things from happening. Interpersonal violence wreaks havoc on the human being. Our bodies, the affective circuitry, the mind, and imagination capabilities are all harmed when we are abused, and neglect is included in the world of abuse. Brain structures and bodies become underdeveloped, sick, or atrophied when abused and neglected.

Reinders and Veltman (2021), in their article "Dissociative Identity Disorder: Out of the Shadow at Last," state that dissociative identity disorder has a known etiology. That last statement bears repeating: dissociative identity disorder has confirmed etiology. Severe trauma is known to create dissociative identity disorder. We know from many studies, using a variety of methodologies, along with fMRIs, EEGs, blood chemistry, clinical and statistical analysis from all over the world, that childhood trauma and torture cause a human being to develop a fractured sense of self along with many other painful, stressful, and chaotic symptoms. We don't know exactly what mechanisms are involved in the creation of a sense of self, but we do know what can injure and break this sense of self. This statement is so significant when it comes to understanding human beings that it should have been front-page news of every magazine, newspaper, and media outlet. This finding is as momentous as the invention of the airplane, the internet, and traveling to the moon, yet too few know this concise and clear discovery of humanity exists.

We know that a child who is forced into any form of sexual objectification or assault, which includes nonphysical molestation, is being so profoundly tortured that everything from epigenetic expression through to the central nervous system, brain development, and sense of identity will be injured and broken permanently without proper intervention. We know this more than we know that lead can cause lead poisoning, yet nothing is ever really done about it. We know that sexual assault against children is the most brutal form of torture a human can experience, a close second to being neglected as an infant.

In several studies, the neurobiochemistry and neuro-bioelectricity of childhood survivors who witnessed domestic abuse were comparable to adult males who have experienced hand-to-hand combat. These injuries do not cause dissociative identity disorder, but they do cause an enormous amount of harm. What does cause dissociative identity disorder is the brutal combination of sexual abuse and parental/maternal neglect, as well as near-death experiences like being choked. We know that childhood sexual abuse and neglect are extremely similar when it comes to the damage that occurs. Child abuse happens in the early stages of development, which is a time when a human is extremely vulnerable and utterly unable to protect or care for themself. Time and again the same information has been found all across the globe: early abuse and infant/child neglect cause catastrophic effects in the developing human. Dissociative identity disorder has been well researched not only in psychology but in other fields of academic study. The fields of attachment and attachment disorders (Bowlby 1977) and the polyvagal theory (Porges 2011) both support and independently find that the early-life torturous experience of assault with genitals and/or neglect harms a human in unfathomably negative ways. Yet grander academia, the Western medical model, clinical training, and media all ignore these facts.

Judith Herman and Bessel van der Kolk (1992) coined the phrase *complex PTSD*, also known as childhood developmental trauma disorder. To summarize, both Herman and van der Kolk attempted to put the most common sequelae of early trauma and abuse into some type of logical phenomenology. These symptoms included suicidal ideation, dissociation, distrust, profound helplessness, hopelessness, substance abuse, self-harm, self-mutilation, feeling socially isolated or socially phobic, difficulty with learning and attention, feeling chronically terrified, chronically rageful, and profound shame. By the early 1990s, the concept of complex PTSD gained clinical validity, and van der Kolk attempted to get the diagnosis of developmental trauma disorder introduced into the American Psychiatric Association's *Diagnostic and Statistical Manual of Mental Disorders* (DSM) fourth edition and subsequent iterations. It never passed. There have been rumblings about the financial implications—and the influence of the pharmaceutical industry—as the reason why this diagnosis did not get accepted into the *DSM*, but I suspect that something else was also at play. It is the same something that has plagued the field of dissociation and dissociative disorders. It is the same something that causes the torture of children to be viewed as some type of normal sexual expression of some people. It is likely the same something that makes us universally assume that men are inherently violent and that most of the violence should get a general pass. It is the same something that classifies this male violence as a simple choice. It is the same something that is very invisible and extremely common. It is likely global and general acceptance of misogyny, driven by the patriarchy.

In the nearly twenty-five years that I have been part of the field of complex trauma and dissociation, I have never heard anyone speak about how misogyny and patriarchy are the root cause of all this strife, abuse, degradation, and psychopathy. I have never heard a plenary talk on how the removal of our first and most important neurobiological affect regulator (mother) might just be the original traumatic wound that leads to so much destruction and devastation. I have never heard a theory of misogyny that makes sense, or even highlights how abnormal all the abuse is. There are discussions on how to help these wounds, but no one talks about the possible source of the abuse, other than being abused. No one talks about how devastating it is for us as a species to not have the accurate regulation that comes from safe/secure mothers. No one discussed how this lack of care leads to massive dysregulation. There are no discussions of what certain humans do when they are dysregulated. There is no real connection to the neurobiological process of needing to harm others to neurobiologically prevent themselves from feeling their own painful, suffering feelings of central nervous system dysregulation that comes from maternal absence or maternal stress. I've heard a lot of theories that excuse these acts, such as males of our species are just hypersexual. Or that these actions and reactions are simply personality styles. None of these theories explain the psychopathic nature of injuring and neglecting a child. I have never heard any leader in the field of complex trauma and dissociation ever speak of the abnormality of patriarchy and how it must be a trauma symptom.

We know that neglect, especially for male infants, can be as damaging and devastating as sexual abuse, yet little is done to change or even address these problems. Male infants are extremely sensitive to maternal stress, and a result of this vulnerability is psychopathy (Schore 2019). It is clear that something very odd is happening. We have these irrefutable facts, yet misogyny is never discussed in trauma circles, conferences, or educational settings. Maybe even the best of the trauma world and the mental health world buys into ancient patriarchal myths of what it is to be a human being. How is it that the one thing that will surely cause massive disruption in human growth, the violent removal of the mother, is not discussed? The one thing known for sure is that traumatic stress affects the brain structures in deleterious ways. When maternal care is stopped or harmed (misogyny) and the forced removal of the father occurs (patriarchy), why is it never considered as a factor to the development of emotional instability? How is it in a profession that claims to be aware of the damage of attachment injuries that the original and continual injury of hating what is considered feminine is not part of the conversation? How is it that philosophical conversations on personality styles and other uber-cognitive musings are being used to explain our suffering instead of a lack of care, compassion, empathy, and attunement? And why is the trauma world not discussing this discrepancy?

Misogyny is not just an invisible trauma; it is *the* invisible trauma. We are a species that evolved unlike any other on this planet. We do not have any self-defense mechanisms like venom or ink. Humans are absolutely incompetent as a singular creature in comparison to the other animals in the natural world. We do not have the speed or strength some animals have. A full-sized, muscular adult male is very weak in comparison to other animals, especially predators. We have dulled senses; our hearing, sense of smell, and eyesight are very poor compared to other animals. Take any human and put them in the middle of the North Pole or near the equator with no clothes, no tools, no shoes, or any resources, and we will die in a matter of minutes, either by the harsh conditions or predation. We are so weak as a species that we can be considered the easily accessible junk food of the African savannah.

Our main defense as humans is other people. Every brain structure and all our reactions that come from the central nervous system are intimately and intricately oriented toward another person or being, as our first line of defense. What makes humans a unique species, even in comparison to Neandertal, is not only our social intelligence but our social survival protection mechanisms. We were made to live in groups of at least 150 people and to be intimately connected, emotionally and physically, with them.

What do you suppose happens to a species whose one and only defense mechanism and main apparatus for optimal growth is violently or taken away forcibly removed? What happens to a creature when the thing that they need more than food—the first person they are neurobiologically intended to interact with—is removed or cruelly annihilated, as is the case in the most misogynist and patriarchal social structures? What do you suppose happens to an infant whose body gets punished for attempting to attach? We know for sure that attachment disorders lead to the development of physical problems, mental problems, learning problems, immune problems, bonding problems, and a whole host of other devastation happens, possibly leading to psychopathy and other disorders of catastrophic attachment failures, such as narcissism or borderline personalities.

The human infant is the most vulnerable creature in the known physical world. Infants and children are extremely vulnerable to predation for at least a full decade, if not more. Infants are unable to feed themselves, walk, move, burp, or pass gas without help. Their little central nervous systems can't even fall asleep on their own. Humans are incapable and incompetent for the first fifteen years of our existence. This glacial-paced developmental trajectory is gargantuanly delayed compared to all other mammals, including our closest evolutionary cousins. We are designed to be taken care of by not just one person, but many, including our fathers. We know that human beings do not start to use cognition until we are at least three (Schore 2019). We also know that humans can feel and sense at birth, as their affective and sensory motor circuits are nearly fully developed (Schore 2019). These feelings and sensory perceptions are taking place in a body that cannot move on its own; it cannot project or empathize outside its body; and it cannot put words, meaning, or context to its inner sensations and affect. If an infant has an uncomfortable feeling, it cannot comprehend where the source of the feeling is coming from. It can only feel it. An infant cannot intellectualize an earache, a pinch, the cold, heat, the brutal feeling of being alone and disconnected (neglect), or experiences that are exactly like being eaten and penetrated (sexual abuse). Infants just sense and feel. Because they cannot project their awareness outside themselves or conceptualize that an outside source is the cause of their pain, suffering, or discontent, they have only a one-dimensional experience that seems to come from inside them-selves—rather than outside. Because affect, or feelings, is humans' very first language, everything we experience is from this affective place. Feelings are how infants communicate to their caregivers.

When an infant has a need, this need is first felt and experi-enced by the central nervous system (CNS). The body of the infant will, from an instinctive and automatic, hardwired, evolutionary place, send the message of the need via electrical currents through the CNS up to the brain. The infant, through movements and gestures and several specific noises, will communicate its needs. These needs quickly move into affect. Over time, and through these early forms of nonverbal language, the infant starts to learn how to self-regulate, or meets its needs, through the act of being regulated. In other words, by someone else meeting our needs. If the needs become more concerning, the inner sensations and affect will become stronger and louder. Many things concern the infant, and their window of tolerance is not that big. Infants do not know what patience is. Patience comes from many years of learning how to regulate one's body and mind; patience is the realm of the

adult. Therefore, if these needs are not cared for rather immediately, the infant's body quickly moves to a state of distress.
Their CNS will become more electrified and more inflamed. If
these needs continue to not be met, the infant moves to a state
of emergency. This emergent state is experienced as pain. Put
simply, if no one is there to help, infants quickly go into a state
of excruciating pain (Schore 2019). This pain, if never properly
attended to, most likely will grow into a continual feeling of
knee-buckling shame. We know this from studying the roles
played by dissociation and the periaqueductal gray, a vital brain
structure at the base of the brain stem that manages life-threat
neurochemistry and neuro-electricity (and sits even lower than
the amygdala, known as the fear-response center of the brain)
in abuse, distress, and neglect. Shame is a symptom of traumatic neglect. Shame, and the pain that is universally experienced with it, far more than fear, must play a major part in
misogyny, patriarchy, and the development of psychopathy.

Inside the mother and father are brain structures that are
designed to be super powerful communicators and interpreters
of what is happening inside the baby's body. The brain structures designed for mindfulness are the same structures that are
utilized, heavily, by people who are securely attached (Forner
2019; Siegal 2007). These brain structures are not a recent
addition to human evolution; they are an integral part of our
defense mechanisms. These brain structures *are* what make us
human. Within humans, especially well-meditated or securely
attached humans, are structures designed to regulate our fear
responses and help us cope with emotions like terror, pain, and
grief, without losing our executive brain functions such as judgment and planning. There are brain structures whose job is to
stay connected to other humans when we are experiencing
intense affective pain. The ventral medial prefrontal cortex
(vmPFC) and the default mode network, two structures that

take decades to reach full maturity, are capable of an incredible amount of empathic communication, internal regulation, language and meaning-making abilities, and many more prosocial skills, and are dominant when we meditate or are securely attached. By utilizing attunement—the capacity to tune into, connect with, and sense another's inner states—the fully mature *Homo sapiens* is able to literally feel what another person is feeling and then make meaning and put into context these experiences of another. In the case of an infant who is having a need, communicated via affect, a parent should be able to know exactly what that need is and be able to immediately respond to the need, so the infant's CNS can go back to its natural baseline of contentment. Further skills that the vmPFC is responsible for are updating procedurally learned experiences so that what happens as an infant does not carry through to adulthood, differentiating between instinct and intuition, and taking a mental pause. For example, the vmPFC can take the very scary experience of being in two feet of water as a child and update it to a less scary one as we age and develop larger in size, ability, and regulation skills. All these brain structures combined equate to an almost mystical level of communication between the infant's CNS and its parents. Conversely, when the human experiences stress, is afraid, angry, panicked, rageful, terrified, or ashamed, these brain structures do not work well or at all. When frightened or stressed, the parent is not able to communicate well with the infant, leaving the infant vulnerable to dysregulation. This, in turn, leads to the infant having difficulty developing these brain structures.

We are designed to be an alloparented creature, meaning that in our natural habitat at least four to six adults cared for one child. For us humans, we need many to meet our needs. Most mammals only have one or two parents who are designed to meet the needs of their offspring, which makes sense when the offspring reach full maturity in a year or two. With humans, we need many to care for us for decades. That is a mind-bending number of resources put toward one creature for a long time. And it is the biological birthing female, or reasonable facsimile, and her mate, the biological birthing male, or reasonable facsimile, as well as two to four more, who are doing most of this heavy lifting. These are facts that are found inside our brains and central nervous systems.

Instead of thick skin, excellent hearing, speed, or some type of camouflage, our defensive strategies went into developing the ability to be intensely connected, with an enormous amount of empathy and compassion for other people. This is how we evolved, our lifesaving, and rather fascinating, survival mechanisms of knowing how to read the intimate details of another's feelings and sensations.

When we are safe and secure, brain structures thrive. When we are scared, alone, fearful, shamed, terrorized, and enraged, those brain structures involved in healthy, loving interpersonal connection do not fully develop, as is the case with many who are lacking attunement or the ability to calm oneself down. Some parts of the brain can become overused, as with people who use only thinking and are phobic of feeling, or they can atrophy in people we would classify as narcissistic, sociopathic, or psychopathic.

Most people crave being loved and seen. Most people want unconditional, intimate, and profoundly safe relationships. We all crave a type of love that is able to bust through our deepest barriers and protective layers. Humans strive to be met with others who will love us, no matter what, without judgment, who would never reject us or shame us. We all crave a feeling that may not really have words: to be fully loved; to feel like others can provide us with their complete attention and full presence; to be with someone who is open, patient, and tolerant. To be fully seen, cared for, and also liked is a more powerful craving than heroin. It is love and we are built for it. These qualities are what the vmPFC creates. These brain structures that are part of a well-working, fully developed homo sapiens do not grow when we are scared and thrive when we are safe. It is our baseline as a species, and we know this because of how well our bodies work when we are safe and securely attached. When people are being mindful with us, when we are in a state of securefulness (a secure or mindful state of human-to-human co-regulation; Danylchuk 2022) all our biology, physiology, and neurology function really well.

By understanding the mechanisms of dissociation, mechanisms that are designed to reduce or fully anesthetize pain and cognitive awareness, one can start to understand what might have happened that caused misogyny in the first place. Dissociation and mindfulness are rival and polar opposite brain and body functions. In examining these two reactions to two very different environments, we can see, clearly, that misogyny is a neurobiologically violent, fight, rage-fueled reaction to inadequate care after trauma or detachment. Attuned, present, aware, connected, empathic care stops dissociative responses and brings forth the internal CNS inflammation, live-wire, physical, and psychological pain of detachment or trauma, which it is designed to do. This previously dissociated pain of isolation (from an evolutionarily determined need for safety in numbers and protection from death and dying) comes flying out seeking and needing the co-regulation and care. In other words, the care that comes from attuned, present, aware, mindful processes, which humans evolved as a protective mechanism similar in creativity as camouflage, care that is in charge of regulating others, does what it intends to do, manage the feelings of others—except that the feelings of detachment and human-to-human harm are too painful to bear and withstand. Violence is a quick, fast, and "effective" affect-silencing solution to the conundrum of not being provided with neurobiologically attuned, empathic care. Patriarchy we can then define as the continuation of staying in a dissociated state (to avoid detachment pain) by harming others or denying all human care, which leads to the root cause of so much of human suffering. The human being is not supposed to harm other humans, as there are zero backup systems inside us to manage this type of injury—first and foremost, it is people who are our backup plans. People are supposed to help us and scaffold us in times of stress and fear. Misogyny takes all this away, leaving only a psychopathic/patriarchal lens with which to construct our world.

It is only in recent years, since the women's movement in the 1960s and 1970s, that we started to look into the damage that rape, incest, and human to human violence causes. I never would have learned that misogyny is the root of all things that are not okay with humanity, even with all of my other education and research into dissociation and mindfulness, if I had not taken that women's studies class. It is fair to say that misogyny and patriarchy are the root cause of every single thing that is destructive, dysfunctional, harmful, and hurtful within current humanity. If you hate, beat, and rape the thing that you need the most, you will never understand what it is to be truly free as a human. For me, feminism is not just a call for equality; it is a call for the profound safety and security that all people need and deserve.

References

Ananthaswamy, A., and K. Douglas. 2018. "The Origins of the Patriarchy." *New Scientist* 238 (3174): 34–35.

Bowlby, J. 1977. "The Making and Breaking of Affectional

Bonds: I. Aetiology and Psychopathology in the Light of Attachment Theory." *British Journal of Psychiatry* 130 (3): 201–10.

Briggs, E. C., L. Amaya-Jackson, K. T. Putnam, and F. W. Putnam. 2021. "All Adverse Childhood Experiences Are Not Equal: The Contribution of Synergy to Adverse Childhood Experience Scores." *American Psychologist* 76 (2): 243.

Danylchuk, L. 2022. "The Centrality of Care." *Journal of Trauma & Dissociation* 23 (1): 1–7.

Emmott, E. H., and A. E. Page. 2021. "Alloparenting." In *Encyclopedia of Evolutionary Psychological Science*, 210–23. Springer. https://doi.org/10.1007/978-3-319-16999-6.

Forner, C. 2019. "What Mindfulness Can Learn about Dissociation and What Dissociation Can Learn from Mindfulness." *Journal of Trauma & Dissociation* 20 (1): 1–15. https://doi.org/10.1080/15299732.2018.1502568.

Hare, B. 2017. "Survival of the Friendliest: Homo sapiens Evolved via Selection for Prosociality." *Annual Review of Psychology* 68, 155–86.

Herman, J. L. 1992. *Trauma and Recovery: From Domestic Abuse to Political Terror*. London: Pandora.

Holland, J. 2006. *Misogyny: The World's Oldest Prejudice*. Philadelphia: Running Press.

Porges, S. W. 2011. *The Polyvagal Theory: Neurophysiological Foundations of Emotions, Attachment, Communication, and Self-Regulation*. New York: W. W. Norton.

Reinders, A. A., and Veltman, D. J. 2021. "Dissociative Identity Disorder: Out of the Shadows at Last?" *British Journal of Psychiatry* 219 (2): 413–14.

Schore, A. 2019. *The Development of the Unconscious Mind*. New York: W. W. Norton.

Siegel, D. 2007. *The Mindful Brain: Reflections and*

Attunement in the Cultivation of Well-Being. New York: W. W. Norton.

Van der Kolk, B. A. 2009. "Developmental Trauma Disorder: Towards a Rational Diagnosis for Chronically Traumatized Children." *Praxis Der Kinderpsychologie Und Kinderpsychiatrie* 58 (8): 572–86.

Chapter 8

LandBack—My Body as First Territory

A Love Story

Claudia Villacova,
Medicine Wombyn, LCPC

A Wombyn who heals herself, heals her mother, heals her
daughter, their daughters and heals every wombyn around her.
—Unknown

I am a descendant of the Purepechas, from Michoacán, Mexico,
cousins of the Quechuas in Peru, on my father's side. On my
mother's side it is rumored (and recognized in the faces of my
relatives) that we are descendants of Ndeh (Apache) and
Conchos. Both of my grandfathers were Spaniards, and so I am
a Mestiza who is reclaiming and re-indigenizing her lineage.
The Purepechas are famous for never allowing themselves to be
conquered by the Aztecs and fighting fiercely against the
Spaniards. The brave warriors who fought hard for their land
and culture included wombyn. I come from a long female
bloodline of resilient and resourceful warrior wombyn. Tenderness was not allowed under such harsh environmental conditions; church, patriarchy, and colonialism held wombyn by the
throats, silenced and chastised for anything and everything
soma. Wombyn's wisdom, ways of knowing, went underground,

assuring the children survived and traditions protected from the murderous gaze of the white male draped in Catholicism. My maternal grandmother was the community curandero and oracle. Later in life, she would undertake evangelism, just in case it was real, and she was praying to the wrong people. My paternal grandmother, widowed by thirty, raised eleven children and ran a farm without knowing how to read or write. She developed her own way of counting money and keeping business accounts balanced. My paternal aunts all were successful entrepreneurs despite being housewives and not knowing how to read or write. I remember watching the wombyn on my father's side . . . how they walked tall with dignity. On the other hand, on my mother's side, the wombyn were in perpetual longing for a man to love them, like in the telenovelas. Telenovelas were always playing in the background of my maternal relatives. With my paternal relatives . . . long hours of hard work on the farmlands and in the kitchen made no time for TV; they didn't even own one until I was well into my teenage years. The wombyn on my mother's side all had very difficult marriages with some form of domestic violence. The wombyn on my father's side did not. All lived well into their marriages. I connected this to a simple fact. My paternal grandmother was cared for and loved deeply by her mother. In fact, she was her mother's favorite. Her mother's deep love gave her the strength to push through being kidnapped at age thirteen by the man who would become her husband by force. My maternal grandmother, on the other hand, was orphaned at the age of four and roamed around house to house until one day, tired of roaming around as an arrimada (forced unwelcome guest), she made a bet to marry the next man who would walk through the door of a local tiendita (little convenience store). Coincidentally, my father would be taken to a Jesuit orphanage at age six to secure his education when my grandmother became widowed with eleven children and a farm to run. My mother was born to a wombyn not knowing how to mother her. And she married a man who was not mothered by his own mother (although she loved him deeply) and who was severely abused (to get the Indian out) at the orphanage. Both my parents never were able to feel loved, be intimate with themselves, or be able to give love and enter its transformative power. They locked into a trauma bond of abandonment and raged war at each other in a very dehumanizing way. Dragging their children with them. The fact that I was a rebel from the start and was able to survive and overcome my childhood despite being raised by a mother who would remain disempowered and submissive to my father until her last breath at the hands of cancer is a testament to the brilliance of my DNA. I am my ancestors' dreams. I am a seed of love and light, and seeds never die, they survive and thrive when they eventually find the right conditions to loosen the shell and soil to root in.

It took a very long time for me to differentiate from an imposed Western-mind and its hyper-individualistic prism. I was so top-heavy I bought into the illusion of a split between my mind and my soma. I worked and worked so hard to figure out what was wrong and figure out how to fix it. Holding this narrative in the inner landscape of my brain caused a painful incoherence. It took another chunk of time to learn how to consciously inhabit the territory of my body; understand its inherent technology; and have access to my humanity, my medicine, pleasure and ecstatic experiences, as is my birthright. As a wombyn during these times of our human herstory, with a war against wombyn still raging . . . ecstatic, erotic joy, and pleasure through my body is liberatory and a revolutionary act in itself. To activate my DNA and remember it took most of my fifty years of living to locate myself and take my rightful place as a human being, and caretaker of this beautiful Earth. Recognizing myself as a medicine wombyn took many years of intentional presence, curiosity, focus and healing in community. Breaking out of the prism of western hyper-individualism was essential in my re-indigenization as well as my re-humanization. My healing journey has been mostly about removing what was foreign, artificial, and oppressive living within me, while surviving in an overculture, with a particular kind of hate directed at Mestizos like me, people who were born to parents born in Mexico and migrated to the U.S.A. for a better life for their children. To grow up in a country that labels me a second-generation immigrant, when my ancestry comes from these North, Central, and South American continents by European immigrants who claim to be from here, was (and continues to be) very damaging. This form of gaslighting, paired with an educational system that removes my history and the history of this land from their curriculum while centering European history, from kindergarten onward, was the core of the toxicity I had to identify and learn to unlearn. And so, ... my healing journey is a story of love and trust, with love of myself at the center. To get to my self-love ... I had to dive down into the depth of my self-hate. I had to learn to trust my not knowing, to surrender into the dark abyss, to sit with my chaos and pain—with wide eyes and curiosity. In trusting the process, my inner wisdom to feel universal love began to flow within me, and I began to learn to fall in love with myself.

To tell the truth, as occupants of this holy land, is an act of love. As I put my body in places where wildlife was intact or intact enough, like the Andean mountains, coasts, and sacred sites of Costa Rica and Mexico, or the jungles in Central and South America, my body and spirit began to remember my own original inner landscapes, unlocking a wild howl of loss, grief, and pain. As I unleashed my cry out to Pachamama ... my blood spilled onto the once borderless soil of my ancestors in agony. I kneeled down the Great Mother in my appeal to heal the generational trauma living in my soma and auric field so I could finally come home. Home to my Body, to my Being, and welcome back my spirit and soul. Little by little ... I reclaimed my heart, body, mind, ecology, and spirit. Like water transforms rocks into smooth stone, surrendering to not knowing and choosing love and learning to love transformed me. A lifetime of unlearning, learning, gathering tools and skills for healing was an act of love for my own sense of home in my own body. A desperation to reenter the sacred hoop and be intimate with myself so I could feel my kin. I can now say, looking back, I was fighting for my life all along, for the right to feel, love, be free, and have self-determination and sovereignty. It took a long time of releasing, forgiving, unlearning, and trusting myself to get to an integration no Western psychology or modern medicine can accurately describe or intellectually articulate. As a thriving survivor of intended Indigenous erasure, I now understand I am a sacred seed, and as such I can never be destroyed and will always have a responsibility to be in service and give voice to the Indigenous communities and the protection of our ways of knowing, rituals, ceremonies and lands, this Earth. Without Ecological understanding and wellness ... we will continue to live in confusion as to what is true and what is real. Without a personal knowing of the Sacred, we will continue to confuse the profane with the sacred, performance with ceremony and ritual. Until we are in the right inner and outer ecological relationship, we will not have personal access to our powerful medicine and heal our bodies. We are the Earth. And my liberation is interwoven with your liberation. As a storyteller and keeper, dreamwalker and catcher, language keeper, rhythm keeper, and circle keeper on this red path ... I fight and heal for your liberation. Even if you hate me, my ways, or my people. I walk and pray for your self-sovereignty because you are my relative. Every living being, all that has Pachamama's pulse running through is my relative and I am one with all of Life. Ajaw.

As an Indigenous descendant, pulling from my own ancestral and cultural Indigenous teachings, I engage health and wellness through the lens of the Medicine Wheel, which is embedded within a complex and nuanced ecological framework mirroring the nature of life and living. There are many interpretations of the Medicine Wheel; my own understanding and interpretations come from the traditions of the Olmecas, Toltecas, and Mayas, as taught to me through dreams, visions, and by abuelos and abuelas (human and spirit beings) from my native lands beginning in Mexico by my own maternal and paternal abuelas, as well as teachings I received during my time in Central and South America. In my interpretation of the Medicine Wheel, as the Universe so the body and soul, as the Great Mystery so the feminine principle, as the Great Spirit so the masculine principle. The Earth has multiple dimensions vertically and horizontally divided in three main parts at the vertical level, which translates into underworld, middleworld, and upperworld. This is also true for us as humans. Within the physical plane we have the elements, Air, Fire, Earth, and Water. In the center of everything, there is an opening, a belly button from which spirit and energetic information comes and goes, moves around within and outside us and all living things in an animated manner. I experience everything as animated, alive, and in movement, everything has a spirit and a "personhood," everything is interdependent, and so I am vulnerable to everything every being does . . . every day of my life, before and after my physical death. This quick explanation is my very basic attempt to present a very complex and nuanced technology, cosmology, and way of putting order to chaos (the presence of all possibilities manifested and unmanifested) to give structure for our establishing a sense of ecological well-being and living on this physical plain.

From this perspective I present my personal journey of Truth, Healing, Transformation, and Rebirth. We all have access to the "river of life," a flow of Life force that is connected to a Universal Wisdom beyond our human comprehension. This power gives us the ability to be conscious, to feel ecstasy, the power of will, desire, intuition and/or body knowing, and the power to act. To be in Motion. And so, for me, my journey has been less about healing, and more about releasing and remembering and reclaiming all the territories of my Indigenous Body, my channels as connector and conduit of eternal Life Force. To liberate myself from imprisonment of holograms from my lived traumas as a Mestiza wombyn living on stolen land, under colonial domi-nation, I had to become conscious and decolonize artificial ways of knowing, understanding, interpreting, and being, which were embedded and living, within the planes of my physical body (which includes mind). And so this story is not just my story, it is my mother's story, my grandmother's story, her mother's story and the story of my daughters and, hope-fully, I pray, not their granddaughters. At the right time, I will intentionally pass on the threads of my lived wisdom, my medicine to my beautiful daughters, as a descendant of an ancient, brilliant, loving and kind advanced technology and tradition. The Red Path. And so they, too, will weave their lived wisdom for the generations who follow, to know herstory as told by me, through our oral traditions true to my people. And so with permission and gratitude to The Sacred Hoop, The Great Spirit, and The Great Mystery, and my abuelos and abuelas, my teachers and guides, seen and unseen, so it is, as it has always been and will always be, in this space before time and beyond time ... as it is spoke by me, a re-indigenized wombyn, through the air ways, into your ears and heart, in service to the Sacred Heart. Ahaw.

As young as five years old ... my dreams were my main guides from the Spirit world, they never left me ever. They have been my faithful companion on this pilgrimage. When visiting Mexico and here in the U.S., my maternal grandmother would greet me upon waking with coffee mixed with condensed milk. I loved my abuela's coffee! I remember holding the warm clay mug in my small hands to feel the warmth against the coldness in her adobe house with no heater. We would talk about my dreams. She would listen very attentively, didn't really give me much instruction, she was present, nodding while asking questions. Inadvertently, she schooled me in using inquiry to lean into my instinctual knowing. She taught me to love my sleep time and my dreamtime. My abuela, Cuca, was a pueblo appointed curandera. Native to the lands of Chihuahua, Chihuahua, Mexico. I was her "go get" ñieta (granddaughter), "*Claudia!* ... go get me an egg from the chickens, go get me the cup of water bathing in the sun, and bring yerbabuena (healing herb) from the garden." Although it would be decades before I would understand my curandera tools, my dreams, imagination, literature, and storytelling became my most intimate companions and guides. My abui Cuca fed my creative spirit and nourished my soul. She was tender and I felt loved. Unfortunately, I only saw her for short periods of time growing up, but it was enough to buffer the horror at home.

Looking back, I remember struggling with parenting my firstborn. My whole life, my mother was unavailable and stuck in an obsessive longing for my father to love her. She put me and my brothers in harm's way to my father's abuse. She never defended us, took responsibility for her life, or left him. She endured dehumanization and extreme misogyny. Mostly in silence. Often taking it out on me with indifference and withholding. Once while training my voice back, a teacher responded to my frustration about how awful I sounded with, "Of course you sound the way you do. How else are you going to sound after holding your breath in fear for most of your childhood and well into adulthood?" This somatic witnessing broke me down into tears. For a long time, whenever I practiced my voice in preparation for ceremonial singing, I would break down overwhelmed with compassion to all the parts of me, all the different ages I was holding my breath in fear, and I would become critical and punish myself for not connecting, incoherent, not getting it, or feeling dissociated. I experienced extreme physical and emotional pain and suffering, feeling her indifference toward me. At the same time, I repeated her pattern with my father by waiting for her to love me, to touch me tenderly, to be my mother. I was frozen waiting for her to pick me, and entered relationships with this wounding until I cracked the code. At fifty, my body still goes through periods of remembering and releasing grief and despair of not having my mother's love intimately touch me—memories I experienced during my preverbal years.

Having a mother who was preoccupied and not rooted in her own body-wisdom also inhibited my ability to learn how to securely connect to another human for a long time. To be able to be open and tender to receive the presence or gift of love from another. To make things worse, my father's dismissive attachment style, with bouts of rage and physical punishment as discipline, caused real harm to my very tender, vulnerable, developing nervous system, severely impacting my ability to have a coherent sense of myself, others, or the world, as well as my ability to have object permanence to soothe my own nervous system. My father was controlling and physically violent toward us. I survived domestic violence but it left lasting imprints on my young, tender brain. I did not grow up with a sense of safety, nor have internal consistent experiences of warmth, pleasure, and joy. I grew up in what felt like a war zone. Thank goodness for my abuelas, a handful of peers, and my very colorful and vivid imagination. Nonetheless, I was a wild and willed child who knew her normal was not normal and wanted to explore what else was out there. I deeply knew there was a better way. For survival, I identified with my father and internally rejected my mother. I had big dreams and visions; being passive and collapsed was not going to get me anywhere. So I made a choice. I took on, head-on, the power manipulation of my father, regained some of my power, and moved out at age nineteen. Eventually water levels out, and it did for me. I often say I was born into a culture of Hate, to a family caught in a horizontal war born from colonial and religious oppression and the toxic disempowerment it creates. My parents were displaced refugees of an unacknowledged ethnic war for the privileged to steal land. Their resilience, however, remained strong without any resources. And as it is true in the wild, the medicine grows next to the poison; when we ingest poison, we create the antibodies. However, one must encounter a visit with death to have access to the medicine. If I am a medicine wombyn, it is because I also am the poison. I had to descend into my death, weave myself back from the scattered, dismembered bones and flesh, and sing myself back to life ... one ceremony, one ritual, one moment, one human encounter at a time.

A Time for Gathering

I came to this planet whole and complete—this I know. Equipped with my creative fire and brilliant storytelling abilities, which gave me access to language and logic, I became aware people liked what I had to say and wanted more. My loving, generous, giving spirit was magnetic, and it appeared people would recognize their truth as I shared my truth. Not having securely attached to my mother, or any nurturing caregiver, I was primed to attach to my intellectual abilities in a robust and creative way. My spirit was safe and struggling, but mostly unconsciously. I kept pushing through with muscle and blazing might. I obtained my graduate degree in clinical psychology with a counseling specialization, while raising two children, with an emotionally unavailable husband who worked and traveled more than he was home. I ran three marathons, qualifying for Boston at my first one. I also took a deep and rigorous dive into holistic modalities of healing: Earth-based traditions, meditation of different schools, yoga, ayurvedic, authentic movement, embodiment practices, and the like. My thirties were a time of hunting, gathering, and healing safely. Eventually my search to heal into my own body led me into my own cultural and Indigenous Earth-based traditions, including plant medicine. My entry to master plants within ritual and ceremony in a community setting led by Medicine people would be the catalyst to disrupt patterns I couldn't touch, to then be able to tie it all together. Although I grew up surrounded by the colors, textures, and sounds of my culture, with curanderismo, dreaming, and spirituality in the water I drank, I centered my attempts to make sense of my chaos and family trauma through the lens of a European-centric psychology. I relied on psychology to define for me what mental health was supposed to look like and how to get there. It gave me seeds, and it also imposed its own type of trauma. I kept thinking I had to figure it all out, when all I had to do was accept the truth I felt in my body and surrender to the exhaustion of thinking I knew.

As I attempted to heal and bring coherence to my mental field, diving into Gestalt, psychodrama, play therapy, narrative therapy, attachment theory, transpersonal, Jung, Freud, Satir, and others proved to be excellent tools. Of course, what spoke to me most were traditions that had remnants of ancient Indigenous practices. Shadow work, unconscious work, and writings around the wild feminine archetype, as well as dream analysis, helped me understand Western psyche and cosmology, giving me a deeper understanding of its colonial impact on my own psyche. I began to discern what kind of mind control I was under. A white-European-American mind control, and it wanted me dead, sleepwalking, and enslaved. Slowly, I began to be able to map my thought patterns and belief systems, as well as those of my family system, gaining the ability to discern and recognize what was artificial, foreign, and not based on fundamental universal truths. I began to hear my own personal truths. I devoured books on neuroplasticity, neuropsychology, brain and the nervous system, biology of the cell, anatomy, all the way through graduate school. I began to understand how Western culture had clashed with my Indigenous/mestiza science with thousands of years of practice. This brute takeover had devastating effects on my psyche and overall health.

The more I relied on logic to understand my trauma and dissect patterns, the more codependent I became to my intellect to make sense of my world and predict a way into a healthy future. I was convincing myself there was a way to fix me so I could function inside a racist, misogynist, and gaslighting over-culture that hated woke wombyn. Especially woke brown wombyn. Meanwhile, my body began to shut down. My body pushed me out. I became hyper-intellectual, unable to trust what was out of my intellectual reach. Eventually I realized I was killing my own feminine. I was reenacting what I was conditioned to do, what I watched my father do to my mother. Distrust, silence, dismiss, disempower, and erase the wombyn I am. Unconsciously my internalized toxic male wanted to kill her if she did not succumb into obedience and become an object, of a male-desired version of female. Never a real person. The soft animal of my body hardened, turning further inward, locking me out further from my own body territory. I began to mimic and inflict my father's puritanical, piercing gaze, demanding full access to my inner workings. Drowning in my search for truth, control of my environment, and speedy access to innate gifts, I was forced to face my internalized toxic, invasive, white patriarchy under the guise of psychotherapy. My body began to act out, rebelling against my determination to "fix myself." Fortunately, in my moments of clarity and despair, I dropped onto my knees, into my dark emptiness, and cried for help ... and was heard.

By my late thirties, I began seriously exploring breathwork, drumming, astral travel, shamanic journeys, and channeling. I poked and dabbled at many different traditions before stumbling back where I started, beginning my homeward journey. I was attending a psychology and psychotherapy conference in California. A few wombyn curanderas there offered to unofficially open the conference with a ceremony rooted in their tradition. I was invited. The ceremony grabbed hold of me and opened me up in ways I am still understanding. After the ceremony, I decided to attend a workshop one of the curanderas was facilitating. Moved to tears, I began to remember. After the workshop, I went up to the abuela curandera and shared how my grandmother had always told me I had the ability to heal with my hands, but that I had chosen psychology instead. She warmly looked deep into my brown eyes, with a stillness which seemed to stop time and bring me into the present. "Well, what do you think this work is? It is healing work, great job in choosing this entry point!" Just like that. She proceeded to teach me a song—"Corazoncito." It was my first medicine song I used in ceremonial circles with wombyn. ... I still sing it today in ceremonies. I feel white Europeans will never truly understand the impact that being sent to schools centering white European Americans' ways of knowing has on our felt sense of our own ways of knowing and healing, cultural identity, and inner ecology while living in a society that actively attempts to erase our true herstory of this land and its people. The depravity of a deeply rooted spirituality and ecology as a norm in this country still hits me violently on a daily basis.

As a brown, mestizo wombyn, innately collective in my values, I had to dig deep and find myself in a climate of hyper-individualism and artificial knowledge about the nature of nature. Pulling myself up from my own bootstraps, self-healing, and all the messages of "fix it" within a sterile sense of aesthetics, values, and morality (along with my trauma) helped create a very punitive inner critic, fearful, and rageful of my own humanity. It pains me to remember how disorganized, fragmented, and incoherent I was while trying to stay sane. I was attempting to do it all, while internally falling apart. I was rewarded for this and moved up professionally. To have an abuela, established and "professional," see me and tell me I was indeed a healer … impacted me to my marrow. It gave me permission. I began to believe in my healing abilities. Maybe I was not a fraud. Maybe I was capable. I began to imagine the Universe was listening to me, and I had the power to communicate with it and ask for what I needed. I prayed, "Please send me a teacher, I am ready to learn." Within a week, I met a wombyn at an event and who connected me to who would be my meditation teacher and energy healer/teacher.

Within a month, I was studying kriya yoga through the yogananda tradition with a well-established teacher and community. Oddly enough, yogananda, unrecognized to me at the time, had previously visited my dreams a few times. We were having a grand time playing together. I began working with Abby, a very skilled somatic energy worker as well. I had always been able to read the signs, feel the waves and hear what was coming through the airwaves—more and more I began to trust in my intuition and channeling abilities. I sensed I was in the right place and on the right path. And I was.

As my body continued to shut me out, my ability to hear my channels and connection to Source went underground. I had been force-pushing forward at a very high speed, hardening, and tightening my holding patterns and breathing patterns. My unprocessed emotions began to bleed and wreaked havoc on my body. My gut began to sound off loud bells. My gut was in very bad shape, which caused problems with my drainage systems as well as my biochemicals. As I learned to hold images (object permanence) through kriyas, breathing patterns, and other meditative techniques, everything began to erupt and come out of my pores. The more I practiced sitting and focusing. The more rage I felt. Mostly I felt rage toward my then husband, and at myself. As I practiced and practiced. Rage turned to pain. Abby worked on my energy patterns and muscle memory for five years, attempting to release generational holding patterns long enough for me to remember how to reconnect me with my eternal flow of Life Force.

As I began to heal, Abby and I became friends, and she taught me energy channeling during that time. I began to learn how to tap into energy patterns, pull on them like strings in midair, hold them in my body, and to introduce them into the body as alternatives to the energy patterns causing havoc in my physical systems. How to manipulate frequencies, how to travel back in the body's recorded herstory. To be able to pull through a skill for the ability to use in the now—absolutely blew my mind. My body's intelligence could track her and absorb her medicine. Energy work captivated my curiosity and fed my very hungry mind in a fun and pleasurable way. My healing and medicine began to accelerate and develop under the gentle and wise guidance of Abby. My meditation community also contributed in a foundational manner. I picked up skills that would prove to be essential later when I would be initiated into my medicine through plant ceremony.

Looking back, I can clearly connect the dots; moving through, it all seemed unconnected, fragmented, dissociative and without form. My beautiful spirit and guides, of all kinds, never left my side and continued walking with me as I began to organize my sense of self, body, heart, and spirit. I began to study to be a yoga teacher and dived deeper into intentional movement with prana, to begin to feel my body intimately, and eventually attach to my own soma. It took a long time before I could enter and share intimate space with my own body. I was learning. I could bring it in with my client work and with my children (to some depth), but it would be a very long time before I could experience the joy of feeling embodied intimately and connected with another body to explore and experience deep tenderness, trust, secure attachment, and begin to experience pleasure, sexually and emotionally. The old me, the old way of sensing, my intimate roadmaps and mental pathways, had to die. What slowly emerged was so beautiful I would go through days of such deep sacred vulnerability and gratitude. The stories of harm became more round and the humanity of my husband, my parents and so many loved ones became more clear for me. My deep sense of forgiveness to myself for the harm I had caused, my role in their suffering, opened up so much space for love to flow in. The Universe is so generous and we are so loved. Every single one of our cells ... is pure love.

I would encounter my own death while learning to cultivate an intimate personal relationship with death herself. Learning to understand the life/death cycles helped soften my fear of losing my mind as I entered the painful thresholds of transition and transformation. My abuela Cuca would often repeat, "Si quieres aprender a vivir con pasión y gozo, tienes que aprender a morir muchas veces, venimos a perderlo todo, menos el amor, eso si no lo llevamos con nosotras más allá de la muerte." If I wanted to learn how to be alive, I would first have to learn to die, over and over, for we come to learn to lose it all, except love, love we take with us beyond death. And so, a big death did come knocking at my door and thus began my conscious relationship with la Muerte, which led to a conscious relationship with Life and an intimate relationship with myself. Death brings in new life, and so it was true for me.

The Descent into the Underworld

I was married with two daughters, a nice home in a very affluent part of Chicago, graduate-level education, children in private school, ability to travel internationally, three marathons under my belt, a very active social life, PTA meetings, my family, I was go, go, go, go until I began to slow down to Earth, my body ... and then the diagnoses. My mother had stage IV breast cancer with two years left to live. My world began to spin, at first slowly, as I caught up to myself, it began to spin out of control. I had accomplished it: the American Dream my parents had sacrificed so much for their children to have. At a glance, I was the only one who had completed post-graduate studies, had "financial security," a supportive husband, and a healthy family. Now when I look back at pictures from that time, I don't recognize myself. On paper, I was successfully doing all the things I was supposed to do as an adult in this country, living the American Dream while sleepwalking and numb to most of it. My heart closed off and my spirit domesticated. I was composed.

I learned to think about my feelings, analyze and dissect them into logical, manicured stories I told myself to function. I was passing. My mother's cancer was a turning point. After a few years of embodiment work, death came knocking on my door. I had to face my mother, the mother who was still sleepwalking, waiting for my father to see and love her. I was forced to face the cold truth of not knowing her. I felt estranged and distant from her. I made the decision to tell her I loved her every day. And so I did, as awkward as it felt, as lacking in a feeling sense as it initially was, I told her I loved her. Every day.

This seemingly simple act began shifting my body narrative about my relationship to my mother. It created enough safe inner space for my body to soften. I was able to lean in with curiosity. I began deconstructing some of my somatic trauma memories around my relationship with my mother, stories I carried, and my interpretations of her responses to me growing up. I remember thinking I needed to be conscious and intentional about what I wanted to say and ask my mother before she transitioned. Unconsciously, I was attempting to control how much pain I would be left with after her death. But life had its own plan. One morning, after she had transitioned into a less conscious state, I felt an impulse to lay next to her. I got into a spoon position, cuddling behind her. As I felt her, a deep sadness overcame me and I began to sob, waves and waves of loss and grief for my mother. The sadness of it all hit me. Broke something in me, or maybe it allowed me to face what had been broken for a very long time. To have had a lifetime of sharing space with my mother and to never have felt her love, know her intimately, seemed so tragic to me. The pain was overwhelming, as I surrendered into it, it touched and brought alive the most tender and young parts in me. As she emerged, I welcomed her and slowly I fell asleep entering my dream state.

I began to enter a dark space, with shimmering light pulling me into its center, I was swimming into a spiral of darkness and shimmering bits of light ... as I reached the center, my mother was there waiting for me. She appeared in shapes and contrasts of light and darkness, with a clear form. She was so beautiful, warm and generously loving; I could discern her so clearly. She gazed into me in silence, as I gazed into her, I could feel no story, no herstory, just love. Love for me, intimately and intentionally for me. She lifted her right arm while extending her index finger to touch my forehead. An overwhelming and expansive sense of love overcame me, "Aqui estoy," she said to me. I am here. I woke up.

As I reentered my physical space, I noticed a softness in me and a brightness in the room. We had both been touched. My mother was more at ease. She was present in her essence. It appeared something had settled; her skin was glowing and youthful. I felt, for the first time, she was with me. I could feel love flowing naturally between us. I sat by her side the next two days, her last days with us. I held her hand until she took her last rattled breath. As she released her exhale, I witnessed a beautiful blue light swirl out of her mouth, disappearing into the air above her. She was finally free. Just like that her body was lifeless. I gathered the grandchildren, and we began a blessing ritual to prepare her body to release her for her journey back home. An hour later, I witnessed a translucent replica of her physical self sit up, stand, and take a step into thin air. In an instant she was gone. I was in shock.

Within minutes, my youngest brother ran downstairs and told me he had seen our mother walk into her bedroom. Her spirit would circle us for the next sixty days. My daughters would simultaneously have dreams of her dressed in white, frantically trying to communicate something, but they could not understand her. Eventually she would enter her journey, we would all dream of her in white, sitting in a lotus position in silence, eyes closed in peace. The dreams would mark the beginning of a long descent into my own darkness and spaces of shadow. I felt as if the physical anchor that tethered me onto this Earth had disappeared and I was lifting, floating, flailing, attempting to feel ground again and not knowing how. A few months later, a good friend, alchemist, and astrologer said this to me during a birth chart reading, "In ten years you will not recognize your life as you know it now." As I write this, ... it has been twelve years, and my life now is nothing like it was before my mother's death.

".... remember to hold love tight, take it with you into the dark, into all your deaths." Abui Cuca

I remember feeling as if I was intoxicated the first six months after my mother's death. Nothing made sense. I felt like I was looking at everyone and hearing everyone from the bottom of the pool. Yet I was expected to continue as if nothing was wrong by those closest to me, including myself. A month after her death, I attended my then sister-in-law's wedding. I felt prickly, wanting to yell at people. On the verge of tears the whole night. At the wedding ceremony, I remember hyper-focusing on the bride and groom, attempting to sense if they were truly in love. I needed to know if they were truly in love. I could sense their connection and commitment was real; knowing this brought ease to my nervous system. I then began to question my marriage, my mom's marriage, my brothers' marriages. I found so much pain and confusion everywhere I looked. I wanted the whole of the universe to reflect back what was inside me. Everything seemed to be spinning, and I was losing ground quickly. Not only did I question my marriage, I began to question my sexual orientation.

Not long after, I fell in love with the most tender, loving wombyn who shared my mother's birthday. After one kiss, I knew. I was gay. Dazed and confused, I wake up from a gray world and begin to feel, see, and taste color. Love is the most powerful medicine. I fell hard and deep in love with this wombyn. My sensory world became bright with rainbows and brilliance. I began working hard to keep it all together. My family, my new sexuality, my new life. For what seemed like a long time, I juggled holding my husband's hand through the abandonment, emotionally holding space for my young daughters while they witnessed their mother transitioning from completely centering her life around them to breaking loose and wild into a whirlwind of sexual exploration.

I was reclaiming myself, my right to pleasure, my body, taking control of my life. I was breaking free of my marriage, my role as a devoted and self-sacrificing mother, committed wife, and a good and successful wombyn. The wild was calling me home and I stumbled my way back home without hesitation. My years of professional training in somatics, meditation, yoga, attachment theory, energy work, my own reclaiming of my Indigenous medicine, rituals, ceremonies, and traditions were not enough to hold me as I attempted to break out and break through into remembering myself back. I began to feel a very deep hunger and thirst, ... sensing a need to reunite with something much deeper and intimately familiar to me. I decided to partake in an ayahuasca ceremony. It would be the beginning and the end ... as my own mother, I would be prepared to give birth to the wise ancient one within me.

Plant Medicine: Pachamama Takes Me into Her Arms

A dear friend visiting shares her travel plans to Cusco that November. I share my dream. She invites me to join her. A few months later, we traveled. Within a day of landing and installing myself at the lodgings of my friend, I am taken to visit abuela LuzClara living in a small village at the foot of Pachatusan, a sacred Apu in the Andean Mountains within a plant medicine community. Abuela LuzClara and I quickly recognized each other and entered a deep soul connection. After a light lunch, LuzClara instructed me to retrieve my bags from my Airbnb. She had made arrangements for me to stay the remainder of my trip in a house a few steps from hers, and I would be participating in an ayahuasca ceremony that night. She introduces me to Nacho, a medicine man and brilliant world-percussionist and musician. Nacho would become someone near and dear to me, along with his family. I had found my tribe and soil for my seed to root in.

My first ayahuasca ceremony changed the molecular biology of my body. My body's nature and innate medicine was activated. Ayahuasca was a doorway into my body as medicine, my body as instrument, reclaiming my bloodline curandera knowledge, reconnecting to my own sense of my interconnectedness to all of Life, my rhythms allowing me to locate myself and know my inner landscapes in reclaiming my first territory, my body as land. It is well known that ayahuasca can make you vomit. Seems appropriate that the first step to healing from the tight hold of a white European overculture and what it imported onto these sacred lands would be to vomit. I had to vomit. ... all the filth I was taught to believe about myself, what my father was taught to believe, what my mother was taught to believe about herself, and what she had to go without. What my ancestors endured as their sacred lands, and spiritual centers, were destroyed. Many of my ancestors were killed or enslaved into a deep sleep for generations.

I had to purge for a very, very long time before I could even have access to my body, free and clean, and begin remembering I have a right to be here, here on this North American continent, land of my ancestors, here on Earth, here in the Universe. And so began a much deeper and profound sitting practice. Working with abuelas under the Tolteca Maya traditions I began to supplement my plant ceremony work with a recapitulation of my narratives, breathwork and movement, my sitting practice and somatic journaling. After many years of working with Master plants and my abuelas, I began entering sacred relationships with mushrooms, eventually serving psilocybin, and facilitating "velacion" ceremonies for others. Plant medicine is one way ... we can regain entry to our Nature. To a cosmology with information to understand our interdependence and interconnectedness. A roadmap to ecological wellness and health. With the appropriate guidance and integration, in a setting lush with nature, bodies can turn on their innate healing wisdom for guidance into tapping into innate medicine. However, purging and putting new patterns into practice on the physical plain, mentally, emotionally, behaviorally, and physically is essential for transformation. Practice takes time and work and is essential in creating the new structures needed for transformation. Our bodies are our instruments, quite literally and figuratively.

I pray every day for guidance on how to move as a human occupying this Earth grounded in Love. To embody the compassion necessary to face truth wide eyed without blame, shame, or punitive responses to inhumane behavior. I pray for grace, so I see the being in the human gripped in supremacy or self-hate. I am in service to this beautiful, generous land now called South, Central, and North America. May we remember our ways of knowing. May natural law and Indigenous peoples' lives and territories be centered and protected. I firmly believe our innate human nature is loving, kind, and very generous. We are also part of the animal kingdom. We have instinctual drives including a natural predatory nature that is sacred when balanced within the sacred hoop. Although our current social-political climate would have us believe the contrary, the truth is, we are Love. We have the innate ability to heal ourselves in ways that stretch our imagination. It is quite simple, in fact. Our innate healing power has been in practice for thousands of years by Indigenous people around the globe. Modern medicine and Western psychology are young, still in diapers in many ways. Europeans have been studying, documenting, and appropriating Indigenous medicinal ways for hundreds of years. I now know I have always been a water protector and a Medicine Wombyn as much as I am a Lover of all living beings. I know Love is the Medicine and my body the instrument that allows me to tap into the Powers that animate my cellular intelligence, opening the networks living in my DNA. One of the most powerful powers I now have access to is the ability to receive love, to feel loved by other humans and by all my relatives. I always had so much love busting through myself, I knew how to give it away, how to feel it flow through me. I had to learn to receive. Learn to flow what was coming through me to myself as well. To learn how to be intimate with myself and others. To deeply listen. To see with naked eyes and be influenced, touched by the nakedness of another. How to ride and share the rainbow dragon. My bloodline matters. My ancestors left imprints, holograms of their lived stories, oral stories embedded in the fibers of my being, expressing their patterns in the unconscious impulses sending waves across my Mind, Heart, and Body so I could recognize them in nature. All around me. They guided me in my ability to speak, hear, and connect to plants, of all kinds. I am grateful to my oldest and wisest abuelas and abuelos in the plant world, including my most faithful teachers, the trees all around me. We are most like trees. And they love us so much. Each with distinctive personalities, just like us. Here, in this present moment, ... I stop my love story, my mother's story, my grandmother's story, her mother's story, and the story of my daughters, and my great granddaughter's story because it is my story to share and now it is your story too. Ajaw.

Part Three

*Life-Threatening Events
and Healthcare Systems*

Chapter 9

Medical PTSD

The Triple-Edged Sword of Reaching Out with Chronic Illness

Hūhana Jade Barclay,
MCounsPsych, MPH, MBA, PhD

The Promise and The Pain
Every day is a trade-off
between risking and reaching
speaking up or staying safe
living between the promise and the pain

when our very existence is exhausting
is contested
is paradoxical
is unreliable, invalidated, disbelieved

when our health disparities
are so obvious and real
yet so unseen, undocumented, dismissed

when we live between worlds
the kingdom of the sick
the kingdom of the well
invisibly in both

Hūhana Jade Barclay, MCounsPsych, MPH, MBA, PhD

not fully in any

when the burden of proof
the burden of education
the burden of paperwork
the burden of illness
the burden of existing
the burden of inaccessible support
and unavailable accessibility

a thousand extra miles to crawl
before the starting line is in reach

when this life, this world
this perspective and all it brings
the curiosity, the complexity
the insight, the oracles
the comfort with uncertainty
the systemic and unspoken

so obvious in our bones
but oblivious in our books

this precious life
this precious voice
this precious paradox
nestled between the promise and the pain

Medical history is complex. When asked about it, we usually rattle off a list of diagnoses, surgeries, and medications. That's our documented medical history: transactional, billable, an audit trail of evidence left behind by our interactions, decisions, and experiences of trying to take care of this body whenever something went wrong.

Our embodied medical history is our accumulated experiences, interactions, and memories from every hospital, every clinic, every doctor, nurse, and needle. Every time we were dismissed with a curt, 'That shouldn't hurt.' Every time we weren't fully numb at the dentist, fully heard by the triage nurse, fully funded by insurance, fully seen or respected as a whole person rather than a diagnosis on a chart.

Medical PTSD is real, common, and complex. I've heard it a thousand times from real people and (finally) research. It's not just direct physical or verbal abuse, or being restrained or forced to have needles against your will, it's also a product of neglect, gaslighting, discrimination, and systemic and epistemic violence. The way uncertainty and complexity are acknowledged or denied. Whose voice is heard and whose is dismissed, erased, silenced. Directly and indirectly, it shows up in the clinic and the parking lots, with colleagues and family, in the forms we fill out, and splashed across the news headlines. The more chronic conditions we live with, the more intersectional biases we face, the more likely the medical betrayal scars from last time will be there with us in our medical appointments next time. This is The Strange Situation of Healthcare: us and our scars sitting across from them and theirs, hoping against hope that this time they won't abandon us. Convincing ourselves: this time it'll be okay.

Trauma, in medicine, means a significant impact like a broken leg from a car accident. The trauma-inducing impact, however, is not always physical. The people we turn to for help in our most vulnerable moments have the most significant impact on our capacity to reach for help in the future. With chronic illness, we have to reach out for help a lot. Every time we reach, we risk another betrayal. Living decades with fluctuating disability—diagnosed or not—we face endless loss. It might be your memory or your body that goes first, then everything else. Loss of career, routine, identity, and friends. Loss of the hopes that you had for your life and family, on top of the loss of physical capacity. When you reach out for help to people and institutions that want to treat a single organ, a single illness, or a single body part, and yet your body and test results don't match their textbooks and specialties, every visit to a doctor risks compounding the losses, dismissal, and betrayal of every doctor before. Those of us with chronic illness need to understand the overlap of all the different physical and mental symptom cascades, dance around the status quo in the system, and maintain an internal fire of hope that we might get answers this time. Trauma, loss, reaching and risking, uncertainty and paradox, horizons of hope and acceptance constantly ebb and flow in the background of life with chronic illness.

We don't talk enough about coercion in healthcare. Or ableism and inaccessibility in academia. Or clinical relevance and inequity in medical research. During my PhD research, I saw too much of this firsthand, but rarely heard it talked about. The inequity, ableism, coercion, and inaccessibility remain in the system, while the people who see them clearly fall away. "Obvious in our bones, but oblivious in our books." Then survivorship bias kicks in when we only listen to the people who remain, those who the system worked for, those who weren't excluded, silenced, or erased. By not talking about these issues, they too frequently become normalized, unquestionable, entrenched, reinforced, and reproduced. Therapeutic jurisprudence has no equivalent framework in healthcare. The process of accessing justice can be therapeutic, but the process of accessing healthcare is too often unjust. The same is true of healthcare research and funding. People like us are usually excluded from the data and decision-making about research, funding, and services. Our embodied history of trauma, exclusion, betrayal—in medical situations or in life—changes how we experience our relationships with ourselves, our bodies, our health, our world, and our capacity to perceive our own needs, take our own actions, and feel safe speaking up or reaching out.

When a doctor or nurse tells a patient about the tests or treatment, it's not a suggestion. Not really. We talk about shared decision-making, but words like *refused* and *non-compliant* make it into the electronic health record and haunt the patient for life, not the doctor. I don't know if I can handle reading about another young woman with Ehlers-Danlos syndrome choosing assisted death care in the absence of appropriate healthcare. The latest one in Australia was just twenty-three years old (SBS News 2023), but the oldest in Canada was only thirty-seven (CBC News 2023). As more countries roll out euthanasia laws—justified for those who want to make an autonomous choice in the face of an actual terminal disease at the end of a life well lived—more young women are dying with the same medical conditions that my friends and family and I live with. Because the systems they turned to for help made it easier to die with dignity than to live with it.

When something goes wrong, we reach out for help. Sometimes straight away, sometimes we put it off. When it's bad enough . . . When we can no longer ignore it . . . When we get to a place where we can't handle it alone . . . When it's getting in the way of life . . . When the pain of the health issue outweighs the pain of the healthcare encounter.

With a cluster of conditions that routinely set each other off like dominoes, it's often a trade-off between the pain of one treatment and the pain of the inevitable side effect.

But when something goes wrong often enough, when wrong becomes normal, we stop reaching.

Every time we reach out for help, we're inherently vulnerable. And it's awkward. Physically, emotionally, systemically. That awkward interpersonal moment, the dance of discomfort and fragility and uncertainty in every doctor's office. The way we navigate that awkward moment opens or closes possibilities for the next. The power dynamic in the patient-doctor relationship is huge, real, and imbalanced by default, and at least one of them knows it. If there isn't a deliberate process to shift the fulcrum of power, then the doctor has all the power to give life and take it away, and the patient only has hope.

Across all cultures throughout history, toddlers reach up their outstretched arms to adults. This reaching-out movement transcends language and time. By nature, we reach. We turn toward the world and explore, then we turn toward home and reach out to caregivers as a safe haven. If we're tired or frightened or bored or excited, we turn and reach. We reach out to be soothed, regulated, stabilized. We reach out in fear and we reach out in delight. And we learn to survive the response we get from reaching out to our earliest caregiver(s).

When I first heard of the "interrupted reaching-out movement" in family constellations work, it rewired my understanding of myself and my place in the world. Then it came up again in somatic therapy, and again in slightly different terms in Feldenkrais and reading about organismic rights, the borderline mother, and early psychoanalysis texts. Reaching out, turning toward or away, the capacity to be held, to be seen, soothed—it kept showing up everywhere. I realized that it had been there the whole time in the Strange Situation in attachment theory. Mary Main had explained it so clearly with disorganized attachment and dissociation. In Bowlby and Ainsworth's videos we were witnessing patterns of secure reaching-out and interrupted reaching-out movements real-time in the bodies of those toddlers. In my own research, private practice, and life, I'd been witnessing patterns of secure reaching-out and interrupted reaching-out movements real-time in the bodies of athletes and students, executives and researchers, patients and clinicians.

If we learn to survive the unpredictable or negative responses of the caregiver, we learn to expect unpredictable or negative responses every time we reach out. Pretty soon, we stop reaching. The impulse is still there, but the movement is interrupted by default. We see this in toddlers and adults holding their own arms at the elbows. Holding a teddy bear or security blanket or cushion in front of the body keeps us safe in a world that we're not sure can be trusted. It has been given so many names in so many modalities, but underneath it all, it is the same movement. When we're attending to safety and restoring safety in therapy, we're restoring the capacity to reach out that was interrupted.

Every time we encounter uncertainty, explore the unknown, dare to hope for something new, we reach out for help and hope. If we've learned that the safest thing is to not reach out, especially with health issues, that kind of "safety" can get dangerous.

The only time I've felt unguarded in a hospital is when my heart rate was 219 beats per minute (bpm). I didn't have to convince anyone or describe anything. I had a reliable narrator to do that for me—the machines that they know and trust. All my other tests and MRIs over the years have been "normal" (aka false negatives). When in doubt, they tend to believe the machines, not the patient (and working with health AI, I know how misguided this can be). I'd called the ambulance; I'd learned how to advocate for myself, but this time I didn't have to advocate for my health. (I just used those skills to get the paramedics to let me pee before they handed me over to hospital triage, because last time—heart rate 205 bpm—the hospital nurses assumed that my heart rate alone made me a fall risk and wouldn't let me leave the bed to pee.) This is the only time that the tests and imaging and monitors told the story for me. It was just four days after a blood patch, so I was lying down horizontal, and my heart started dancing for no reason. I took a photo of the reading at 190 bpm to show my cardiologist, because my heart is always on its best behavior when I'm in his office. That photo also gave me a timestamp to tell the paramedics later. It turned out to be supraventricular tachycardia and was diagnosed and treated within minutes. The paramedics got me to try to push a syringe plunger out by blowing really hard into it and then rolled me onto my back as my son watched the reading on the machine go from 219 to 90 in one breath. The paramedics called it the Valsalva maneuver. My son called it Control-Alt-Delete for the human body!

Every new diagnosis is a new unknown. But diagnosis isn't always the end of the story, or the start. My ADHD (attention deficit hyperactivity disorder) and cerebral spinal fluid leak diagnoses came thirty-five years after the symptoms started, each with near-instant treatments. My hEDS (hypermobile EDS), POTS (postural orthostatic tachycardia syndrome), and MCAS (mast cell activation syndrome) diagnoses came twenty-four years after the symptoms started. And those diagnoses didn't come with a treatment or management plan—I've had to build that for myself bit by bit over the years. It takes a village.

When I suddenly lost the ability to read, remember, or speak (except in lyrics) in the middle of a grad school class, all the medical tests were normal, but I still couldn't read visually or speak more than four words without singing. Doctors didn't solve that mystery. Patients did. The patients helped me find a unicorn doctor that would recognize and treat the spinal fluid leak that nobody else could see.

Things that doctors (and machines) recognize and freak out about—cancer, aneurysm, supraventricular tachycardia—have had almost no impact or interference in my life. They were annoying but promptly recognized, assessed, and treated. It was the other medical diagnoses that have had massive impact and interference in my life because they went unrecognized, unassessed, and untreated for decades by otherwise well-intentioned healthcare professionals. This kind of patient experience is not uncommon.

My lack of care led to fluctuating disability and poverty, and has been surrounded by stigma, misunderstanding, discrimination, and institutional betrayal in the workplace, which compounded my impairment, both at university and from healthcare and support providers.

Disability, paradoxically, also opened doors to fascinating work that I love, and spurred me to decolonize my thinking and identity. I have re-evaluated my relationship to life, health, work, worth, rest, self, people, and productivity and has helped me focus on what is truly important in life. In that process I have found lifelong friends, collaborators, and mutually enriching personal and professional communities.

When you dive into the ocean in the middle of winter, three things happen. First it stings; even if you knew it was going to be cold, it's still a shock to the system. Then you catch your breath and deal with it. Last, you go a bit numb; you survived the sting. It isn't new anymore, and it fades into the background as you enjoy the ocean.

Every new diagnosis is the same. First it stings.

After the sting it can be refreshing and invigorating to connect the dots in the unsolved mysteries that have been keeping you up at night. This process can make you feel more whole. Not always, but sometimes. After a good swim or a new diagnosis, you feel alive, tingling with clarity and relief. It can open you up to a whole new world of friends who also hang out at the same beaches, ride the same waves, navigate the same weird constellation of specialists and symptoms and side effects and solidarity.

Healthcare ableism is the same. First it stings.

Even when you're used to it, expecting it. Every time I dive into healthcare again, the ableism stings. But this stings like fire, not water. It leaves scars. It is sudden and doesn't happen in just one place. This sting can show up anywhere. It disconnects, gaslights, and fragments us into stressed-out shards of self as we slip through the cracks between the silos.

"What happened?" They glance down at the stick, then back at my face.

It's always the same. Ask, glance down, look up.

I pull out my phone, silently, swiftly flash the photo of my mobility parking sticker like a secret service badge. We were at my grandmother's funeral. I'd been using a walking stick for six years and had been disabled for over two decades. The inquisitive one was my brother.

I'm kind of used to being verbally abused when I park my car. Apparently, I look too young on the outside to be disabled on the inside. At first it stung, but soon became just background noise. It hasn't happened much in recent years, but it used to happen daily, sometimes multiple times a day. Once a guy even came up and bashed on my window while I was still in the car. I understand the sense of justice, I do. I don't think the parking lot vigilantes understand that they are harming the very people they think they're protecting. But all that was before I was using a walking stick. Come to think of it, the mobility aid has become an anti-bias aid as well. I haven't heard a single, "But you don't look sick," since my stick has become an everyday fashion accessory.

Through it all, I've found more and more peace, and possibility comes as we melt the barriers to reaching out. Staying connected as we dive into the unknowns. Connecting with self and community in ways that make reaching out and being reached out to feel automatic, restored, and restorative, once again the most natural thing in the world. Reaching for life, for hope, for goals, for help and health. Learning to find safety and support in new and old ways. We find our way back to ourselves in the paradoxes. Stillness in the movement of the breath. Expansion in the contraction of the heart. Waves of hope and grief, love and loss, joy and pain, pushing and yielding, holding and reaching out.

References

CBC News. 2023. "Why Quebec Fashion Retailer Simons Is Tackling Medical Aid in Dying on Its Shopping Website." Accessed November 9, 2023. www.cbc.ca/news/canada/mont real/simons-video-jennyfer-hatch-1.6641543.

SBS News. 2023. "A 23-Year-Old Chose to Die Today: Australian Laws Made It Possible." Accessed November 9, 2023. www.sbs.com.au/news/article/a-23-year-old-chose-to-die-today-australian-laws-made-it-possible/wx4soya1c.

Chapter 10

The Birth of Healing

Lessons in PTSD Prevention and Resolution from Labor and Delivery

Lisa Danylchuk, LMFT, E-RYT

My Birth Story

My daughter was born after so many hours of labor I have a hard time counting them . . . forty-three? I woke up with contractions early on a Saturday and had the baby Sunday night. As an ultra-runner, yogi, and trauma therapist, I was well prepared for the ins and outs of intense physical and emotional labor and had plenty of coping skills in my pocket. I was even enjoying the ride for the first twelve hours! Then . . . back labor hit, I couldn't pee, and I realized I needed an intervention my midwife couldn't provide.

I had heard enough hospital stories of trauma-*un*informed care that I'd chosen to give birth at home if I could. Early in my pregnancy, I was practically met with a laugh when I expressed a desire to know the doctor who would be there for my delivery. I knew I'd be better off physiologically with a chance to develop familiarity and trust with my primary provider, so I hired a midwife. While the midwife was able to join us as we transitioned to the hospital, she would no longer be the primary provider. Transferring to the hospital was a wild card. While the setting was not one that made me feel warm and fuzzy, it was clear that the higher level of care was in my, and my baby's, best interest. Even with the relational unknowns of the transfer, I felt safe knowing that we would get the care we needed.

Luckily, when I arrived at the hospital on that still Sunday morning in May, I was met with deep compassion and care. The entry staff, security guards, nurses, midwives, and doctors who supported me from intake to exit had gotten the trauma-informed memo. From asking "May I examine you?" to deferring to me on decisions that went against their advice to celebrating me as a first-time mom (rather than using the dreaded term "advanced maternal age"), the skillful and compassionate team guided my daughter and me through a healthy delivery. Staff extended a warm welcome on the way in, and heartfelt congratulations on the way out. What a sweet, deep relief it was for me to feel surrounded by such care.

As a trauma therapist and friend of many moms, I know people do not always receive the connection and care that I did in the hospital. It feels like common humanitarian sense to treat a person giving birth with love, care, and dignity, but there is also solid science to support an approach rooted in connection and care. When we combine awareness of what causes post-traumatic stress with the truth of what facilitates birth, we create a solid foundation for birth support, trauma prevention, and trauma recovery for people giving birth.

What Facilitates Birth?

Physiological birth, it turns out, is initiated by oxytocin. You may have heard of oxytocin referred to as the "love hormone," but you may not be aware of its role in initiating labor. It's even in the name, *oxy* for swift, and *tocos* for birth. Oxytocin is what causes the uterus to contract. It also shows up during mother-child attachment and early feeding exchanges. Perhaps you're familiar with Pitocin? Pitocin is simply a synthetic version of oxytocin that doctors use to induce labor. However, endogenous oxytocin transcends birthing bounds and applies to many universal human experiences.

Beyond birth, oxytocin is released during positive interactions between people, as well as during positive exchanges between humans and animals. It can also be released in response to touch, warm temperature, and food intake. Oxytocin released in these ways contributes to everyday well-being and increases our capacity to handle stress. Food or sex can even be used (or abused) to increase oxytocin and the corresponding feelings of stress relief and well-being it brings. As we commonly see behaviorally, people can seek relief through food or sex in efforts to reduce stress or to compensate for lack of connection. (Uvnäs-Moberg, Handlin, and Petersson 2015).

Being in a state of intense stress or fear can inhibit the birth process, which is likely the reason so many labors stall upon arrival to the hospital—the cold, bright, unfamiliar surroundings a stark contrast to the comforts of home. Birthing centers create environments that feel more like home to support those giving birth in accessing the feel-good flow of oxytocin, thus promoting dilation and supporting the body's natural journey of birth. Feeling disconnection, stress, and fear is directly contrasted with being in an oxytocin-rich state that ripens the body for birth.

The Neuroscience of Healing

In the fields of mental health and trauma treatment, we focus most of our attention on the neuroscience of stress. You've likely learned about how cortisol, norepinephrine and adrenaline, and endogenous opioids play a role in fight, flight, and freeze responses. As a field, we give less attention to promoting positive states and fostering a neurological environment that facilitates healing. If anything, we focus on reducing or managing stressful states rather than cultivating positive ones. Conversations around oxytocin center around attachment but rarely make their way into treatment plan goals or case conferences. Instead of speaking simply about reducing cortisol, we can also encourage states that promote connection and healing. *We can even curate experiences that promote oxytocin in efforts to shift the state and experience of the person seeking to heal.*

The cascade model of defense is one of the lesser-known nervous system models that walks us through a progression of nervous system states as we face an intensely stressful or traumatic experience (Kozlowska et al. 2015, 263). It strikes me that while we have a plethora of models to describe trauma, few, if any, reflect the process of healing. What would a cascade of care look like? It could begin with our body's response to being greeted with warmth, and build as people exchange words, build trust, and hold each other's wants and needs in high regard. In some relationships, physical proximity or touch might increase the flow of oxytocin and the experience of comfort. Unlike approaches to stress hormones, we don't need to shake off the effects of oxytocin. Its presence enhances connection and prosocial behavior, which has numerous positive outcomes for individuals, groups, and communities.

The effects of a cascade of care would indeed be far-reaching, beginning with the body of the person being cared for. Psychoneuroimmunology—the study of the interaction between the mind, the nervous system, and the immune system —helps us understand why many trauma survivors struggle with immune system challenges and syndromes that are difficult to get to the root of. This field helps us learn that traumatic experiences can set the stage for health challenges. When we understand trauma, its impact on the nervous system, and how this relates to every other system of the body, we see how relational harm impacts our cells and our body's ability to thrive. Conversely, relational care, facilitated at least in part by our pal oxytocin, creates an environment that is more conducive to immune function and to healing (Uvnas-Moberg and Petersson 2005).

In addition to psychoneuroimmunology, the field of epigenetics teaches us that behavior and experience matter, and that they have the power to influence genetic expression. In choosing to invest in care, we invest in the future health of the child, which can have far-reaching physiological and social impacts (Merrill et al. 2019). Integrating the fields of neuroscience and epigenetics into the conversation of caring for pregnant people demonstrates how crucial it is that we take a biopsychosocial approach to both birth and healing.

Promoting health and life-affirming physiology for those carrying a child goes far beyond the systems of one body. A pregnant person's physiology impacts a developing fetus, right up to the time of delivery, and beyond for those nursing (Clayborne et al. 2023). By caring for a pregnant person, we care for the child. Keeping in mind the impact of connection and care on oxytocin levels, as well as the mother's psychoneuroimmunological and epigenetic experience, we become aware of the depth of impact social support can have on a birthing person. By facilitating rapport, connection, and a safe loving environment for the person giving birth, we impact the process of labor, and we create an environment of safety for the fetus as well. We can reduce adverse childhood experiences (ACEs) and increase developmental assets that help us access resilience before a child is even born.

Trauma-Informed Care Is Not Laissez-Faire

My personal birth story was full of care, but it was not without moments of concern, or important on-the-spot decision-making. With a wealth of social support, I had plenty of oxytocin flowing, and I also learned more about the kind of trauma-informed care I want to offer.

It is common in trauma-informed practice, and in birth advocacy circles, to defer to the birthing person for all decision-making. Deferring to the person giving birth is worlds better than making decisions for them. Without question, any person giving birth has the right to make decisions about their body. The trauma-informed practice of deferring authority stems from experiences of harm when agency is ignored, stripped, or even ridiculed. These are examples of irrational authority, a dynamic in which power serves to exploit the person subjected to it. Rational authority, on the other hand, "is based on competence, and it helps the person who leans on it to grow" (Fromm 1988, 52).

I am not an expert on birth. In some of the most vulnerable moments of my own birth experience, I craved guidance. I craved rational authority. I wondered . . . What were the implications of each decision? What had these well-versed experts in the room seen that I had not seen? I experienced both the blank stare of someone returning a choice to me without words, and a deep connection when I asked a doctor their professional opinion and they explained to me what experience had taught them, what they recommended, and why.

The trauma-informed practice of fostering agency is not without sharing perspectives, opinions, or expertise. When we are vulnerable, we seek trusting relationships that are engaging and honest. Withholding information or recommendations can be harmful when that knowledge, rooted in valuable experience, could be delivered within the context of rational authority. Being trauma-informed requires honesty alongside respect. Not sharing your expertise and experience can be harmful in some situations, as the person making the decision is restricted from the full scope of information. Building rapport and trust not only facilitates the flow of oxytocin, it also sets the stage for exchanges rooted in rational authority.

Preventing Birth Trauma

I have heard countless stories of trauma-uninformed birth experiences. Ones in which women have been ignored, manipulated, and excluded from making decisions about their own bodies. I've also heard reports of a single word, hand, or eye gaze pulling someone through the most challenging moments of labor. Connection is a powerful tool for strength, resilience, and healing. When we consciously create opportunities for connection, care, community, and relationship, we create an environment that promotes birth and supports growth and healing. When we remove exchanges or actions that involve threat, harm, or exploitation that led to traumatic experiences and post-traumatic stress, we reduce the potential for trauma to occur in the first place.

The cascading effects of trauma or of connection can go either direction, and, with collective awareness, we can reduce experiences of harm and increase experiences of care. By training medical providers in the biological value of care, including trauma-informed principles that promote agency combined with rational authority, we offer an opportunity to improve the birth experience, facilitate genuine connection, and reduce the risks of post-traumatic stress.

When Birth Is Traumatic

Unfortunately, dismissive doctors, unnecessary interventions, infant loss, and even maternal death do happen. Birth is a vulnerable time that is all about the beginning of life, and trauma is connected to death and threatened death (American Psychiatric Association 2022). No amount of connection can prevent tragedy, but it can make a significant difference in healing. When the unthinkable happens, support becomes essential to mental health. Building a base of support for all experiences of birth serves every experience, from the smoothest labor and delivery to the most traumatic loss. Offering connection and relational safety can facilitate birth, ease the strain of complications, and provide a resting space for those dealing with the pain of abuse, grief, and loss. A foundation of care sets the stage for healing in these extreme circumstances, just as it does for those with happy endings.

Resolving to Improve Birth Practice

Within the weeks after my daughter was born, I reflected on my experience, playing over details with amazement—birth is indeed a miracle! One of the pivotal midwives present for the birth, a complete stranger prior to my arrival at the hospital, reached out to follow up with me about my experience. We had a phone conversation, and I was able to ask her questions about the birth, about her experiences as a midwife, and about my recovery. I was also able to share with her precisely what had been helpful for me and why. She thanked me for the feedback and noted that she was a part of an effort to bridge midwifery with hospital-based care. I emphasized my gratitude for her clear, communicative, respectful approach to my birth. It made me feel safe and supported, and I was grateful to have been in such good hands. I remain grateful that people like her are making efforts to improve birthing experiences.

While I witnessed perspectives in my birth education that were pro-midwife, anti-doctor, or pro home birth, anti-hospital, I'm more interested in building these bridges than in falling for the oversimplified game of picking sides. Wherever a birth takes place, it is essential to include a full-circle perspective that integrates the biology of connection and care across birth, birth trauma, as well as trauma recovery. Including awareness of oxytocin, relationships, and connection helps provide birthing people like me with a safe, supportive environment. Beyond simply understanding the physiology of trauma, this awareness provides a foundation of support and healing. Without this foundation, providers and patients alike risk becoming consumed by stress, fear, and the physiological cascade of disconnection. By choosing a cascade of care, we invest instead in the powerful capacity to promote life and healing that each of us carries within. When we prioritize connection, we can more easily prevent and resolve trauma. By choosing deep care in birth, we create a safe space for the child entering the world and offer women better access to trauma prevention and healing.

References

American Psychiatric Association. 2022. *Diagnostic and Statistical Manual of Mental Disorders, Fifth Edition, Text Revision.* Washington, D.C.: American Psychiatric Association. https://doi.org/10.1176/appi.books.9780890425787.

Clayborne, Zahra M., Wendy Nilsen, Fartein A. Torvik, Kristin Gustavson, Mona Bekkhus, Stephen E. Gilman, Golam M. Khandaker, Deshayne B. Fell, and Ian Colman. 2023. "Positive Maternal Mental Health Attenuates the Associations between Prenatal Stress and Children's Internalizing and Externalizing Symptoms." *European Child & Adolescent Psychiatry* 32 (9): 1781–94.

Fromm, E. 1988. *To Have or To Be?* New York: Open Road.

Kozlowska, K., Peter Walker, Loyola McLean, and Pascal Carrive. 2015. "Fear and the Defense Cascade: Clinical Implications and Management." *Harvard Review of Psychiatry* 23 (4): 263.

Merrill, Sarah M., Nicole Gladish, and Michael S. Kobor. 2019. "Social Environment and Epigenetics." *Behavioral Neurogenomics* 42, 83–126.

Uvnäs-Moberg, K., Linda Handlin, and Maria Petersson. 2014. "Self-Soothing Behaviors with Particular Reference to Oxytocin Release Induced by Non-noxious Sensory Stimulation." *Frontiers in Psychology* 5, 1529.

Uvnas-Moberg, K. and Maria Petersson. 2005. "Oxytocin, a Mediator of Anti-Stress, Well-Being, Social Interaction, Growth, and Healing." *Zeitschrift Für Psychosomatische Medizin Und Psychotherapie* 51 (1): 57–80.

Chapter 11

Spiritual Issues and Approaches to Healing Extreme Trauma and Grief in Therapy

Eileen Aveni, LCSW, LMSW, ACSW, BCD

I am a therapist for complex trauma survivors who have sustained ritual abuse, torture, mind control, and spiritual abuse. I didn't set out to have this career, but I have realized that all the experiences that I had in my life prepared me for this extreme and arduous level of work. I can remember in second grade asking God, as I knew Him then, for wisdom. Did I even know what wisdom was? I saw a little child's prayer booklet with a wisdom prayer in it, so I decided to regularly ask for it. All of us ask why difficult things happen and what they're supposed to teach us. I see now that we don't grow unless we are challenged. It may require stepping up and being brave. I believe that we must confront and conquer struggles because they threaten to sabotage the mission we are called to do in this life. Having wisdom equipped me to evaluate each twist, turn, and challenge—and to measure how these experiences might prepare me for the next steps in my life.

Sometimes, however, negative forces are also at work preventing us from fulfilling our call. When that happens, I usually think that if there is so much opposition, then I must be on the right track. Did I want to go another way? Absolutely. Was I at peace choosing another, maybe easier way? No. Was I equipped to fulfill that call? Looking back on my career, all along the way I was being given tools and truths that equipped me for later, more challenging work.

I offer my story to both therapists and others. Whether we are called to therapy or some other line of work, we must not be afraid of hard situations in life. Hard experiences have the capacity to chisel out our hearts and help us develop deep compassion for others and for ourselves—if we let them. Let me show you how I came to cherish this truth for my life. I didn't start out wanting to be a therapist. Not at all. I studied to be a professional opera singer and music educator. But I also loved psychology.

Formative Experiences in My Life

One of the earliest childhood experiences that impacted me profoundly was observing my uncle. He served in World War II and had "shell shock," now known as post-traumatic stress disorder (PTSD). His behavior was loud and brash. It left me puzzled in my young mind. I wanted to understand his story. I watched his children become deeply affected by his frequent arguments. My parents continually reached out to love these children. Today they cherish my parents as loving anchors in their childhood chaos. My parents were role models for me to be ever-patient and loving when dealing with adversity.

As a teen, I was a candy striper at a state hospital for physically disabled adults and volunteered for Head Start in inner-city neighborhoods in Pittsburgh. I was chosen for a life-changing, five-week mission trip to South America with other musical teens. Serving others taught me that people want to be seen, known, and appreciated. I also discovered community and felt a purpose for my life. Working together helps us make more of a difference in people's lives.

College Years

My quest to know my calling took me through a music degree. Music was my passion, but it didn't help other people in the ways that I wanted. So I took a summer theology class which required that I reside in the inner-city living on food stamps, start a new program for that community, accompany a protective services social worker as she evaluated child abuse calls and advocated for children, and write a paper on it. This course challenged me to examine my skill sets and my heart. What was I really meant to do with my life? Later, I completed a second undergraduate degree in psychiatric music therapy, which ushered me into the psychiatric world. An awesome six-month music therapy internship at the University of Michigan Psychiatric Hospitals opened my eyes to the heartaches of patients who were trying to cope with mental illnesses. I trained alongside medical and psychiatric residents, as well as people in other disciplines. I loved it. It confirmed that I wanted to work in the field of psychology.

Beginning My Working Years

My first job was as a music therapist in three psych units of a veteran's hospital. There was complex trauma everywhere around me as Vietnam vets were coming home at the end of the war. Some had been in Operation Babylift—Vietnamese babies being shoved onto planes by their mothers, knowing they most likely would never see them again but hoping for a better future for them in the US. I saw vets jumping over sofas in the day room like they were flying into foxholes whenever someone just opened the door to the room. I was able to design a music therapy program to reach these vets. It was very rewarding, but it wasn't enough for me. Being a music therapist didn't give me enough autonomy and freedom to be in charge of decision-making for a case. Instead, I had to abide by the team's collective decisions. Somehow, I knew that I had a slightly different call in my life. What was it? Could I or should I pivot away from music and toward a total focus on psychological treatment? My identity had been wrapped up in music, but I was finally finding my voice beyond using music as my primary language.

Back to School–Graduate School

I applied for my master's in social work at Wayne State University in the inner city of Detroit, Michigan. I chose this university because it felt more real to me, immersed in the city and all its gritty problems. And from my earlier life as a volunteer, I was comfortable being in the inner city.

I had three internships as part of my master's degree. I first interned at the Forensic Center in Ypsilanti, Michigan, the only one of its kind in the nation at the time. I was training to evaluate men who had committed heinous crimes, to help determine if they were guilty, not guilty by reason of insanity, or guilty but mentally ill, and then treat them. I met pedophiles and mass murderers. These were some of the most dangerous men in the country. Every morning my supervisor and I watched as police cars and an armored truck pulled up with the latest accused criminal wrapped in handcuffs and, usually, chains. If I saw a news report that a mass murderer or some other heinous criminal had been caught somewhere in the country, they would show up at our door the next morning. I struggled to understand them. I would look at their charts and read about the crime(s) they had committed. I remember walking across the day room of a unit or down the halls with men just sitting around watching me walk. It was chilling. How in the world was I supposed to effect change in this kind of patient? At the Forensic Center I trained to be an expert witness, alongside other professionals in the facility. We staged mock trials and drilled each other to know how to answer questions and handle ourselves in court.

The following semester I was placed at the main Child Protective Services division in inner Detroit. My work there dovetailed nicely with the training I had received earlier. (Later I would also earn a certification in child treatment.) In the second year of my master's degree, I was assigned to a child and family service agency to do marriage and family counseling. I was young and not married at the time. I was used to dealing with people who had been victimized by traumatic events. Relating to people struggling with extramarital affairs and other difficult life choices was a new skill for me. There I learned that most people eventually regret their bad choices if given the time to sort and grow through them. I also learned that there are reasons for bad choices. They are very often rooted in difficulties people experienced in their families of origin. I started to develop more compassion. Toward the end of my master's degree, my university supervisor suggested that I consider hospital social work, particularly hospital emergency crisis work due to my ability to think quickly and intervene creatively in difficult situations.

Fulfilling Work Years That Stretched Me

I landed a full-time clinical social work job in a large medical center in Ann Arbor, Michigan, in the surgical intensive care unit, intervening with families of head trauma victims and brain cancers. The ICU patients tended to remain comatose until they were transferred to a step-down unit. I worked with the top neurosurgeon in the region, who had trained under one of the original ten neurosurgeons of the world. He brought me into cases to learn what he did in surgeries. I gained a deep respect for this man. He told me once that operating on the brain was like going into "no man's land." Every time he came out of surgery, he would meet me at the patient's ICU bedside and check all four limbs and all their reflexes to make sure that he hadn't done anything unforeseen to his patient. I learned that life was fragile.

Occasionally I covered the rehabilitation unit filled with fresh amputees, paraplegics, and quadriplegics. I covered heart surgery cases part-time. Heart surgery back then was very risky, so social workers were routinely assigned to all cases. Some patients died on my watch. My social work director noticed that I liked focusing on the actual patients and not so much on the families of ICU comatose patients. She suggested I apply for a full-time job opening in oncology. Oncology patients at that time were always hospitalized for their treatments, so I could get to know them over time. This was a game-changer. I loved it! And it opened the door to my life's work.

Oncology in the early eighties meant that many patients died from their cancers. Some sooner than others. I decided to focus mostly on patients who were between the ages of eighteen and forty-five years. This age range usually had the least support from their peers. Since so many were going to die, I helped some local nurses formally organize a home hospice. I wanted my hospital patients to be able to die at home if they wanted to.

After beginning this work, I realized that I was constantly surrounded by dying people and their loved ones, all desperate for help to deal with their fears, their marriage problems, family feuds, childhood traumas of their own that had never been addressed, child custody issues, spiritual issues, and other family problems that come with someone in the stage of imminent death. I became overwhelmed. I was losing about three patients a week. These were patients I had gotten to know well. I knew their inner struggles and fears. I realized that, in some ways, I was filling the role of a priest in a confessional. When they didn't know how to confess or talk about issues with our staff chaplains, they confessed to me. They told me their regrets about their lives. They questioned spiritual things with me, where they were going when they died, and why God wanted to take them so young in life and leave loved ones behind, especially their children. It was heart-wrenching. I came home at night with what we now call secondary post-traumatic stress building inside of me. I was feeling increasingly desperate. I cried out to God. I loved this job, but how could I cope with so much trauma? Miraculously, I was led to a book by hospice legend Dr. Bernice Catherine Harper—*Death: The Coping Mechanism of the Health Care Professional* (1977). Her research uncovered that healthcare professionals reach a threshold of pent-up feelings by the end of their second year of terminal care work. They either learn how to regularly and effectively grieve these deaths, or they leave the field early in year three. I loved my work, but I was dying inside. I have always been someone who could easily grieve, but the regular assault on my senses from death after death was something that few could prepare for.

Harper taught that terminal care professionals usually store feelings after each death and that you can't possibly grieve every death. One obvious sign of this was starting to get short-tempered with people. That was happening to me. She recommended sitting down with yourself every two weeks and choosing an obviously sad movie, book, or sentimental song to evoke some tears. Once your feelings start coming, allow yourself to switch over to the sad feelings of the most recent deaths that impacted you. She reasoned that once you open the floodgates of feeling, a rush of recent emotion can come forward (Harper 1977). She was right. Each time, I was able to get to a place of outright sobs for each of my patients who had died in the last two weeks. It felt like I had cleaned out my soul every time. I was able to remain soft inside, stay easily focused, and was always ready to attend to the next very sad case and be really present for them. Learning to grieve like this saved my sanity, and it preserved my love of being with these noble patients and staff.

I attended a four-day conference in Chicago called Grief Counseling and Grief Therapy by J. William Worden, which he later published in a book with the same title. Worden was part of the longitudinal study called the Omega Project at Harvard. He differentiated between grief counseling and grief therapy and further defined what grief therapy might look like. He defined "complex grief"—a new term in the field at the time. This conference pushed me to feel grief as my clients would feel it and thereby learn how to treat it.

Grieving Is Key to Recovery from PTSD

I was beginning to realize that grieving was the key to resolving my patients' emotional pain, even physical pain, both in their present lives and in their past. I started to ask my patients at the bedside if they had ever endured other challenging things in life. How did they cope with it back then? Together we explored what worked and what didn't work for them. Would those coping skills work now, or did they need to think about different strategies that may work better? As we worked together, we would usually get to the grief that lay underneath. As we unearthed those earlier unresolved experiences, my patients felt emotionally better. And sometimes their cancers would also recede! At that time, we didn't know much about how the mind and body are connected. The research was just starting to surface. I just knew that *learning to grieve* was another powerful tool that would serve me in the future.

It was 1981, and I was starting to find my voice. A hospital colleague brought *I Can Cope*, an educational program for oncology patients and their families, to Michigan from Minnesota, where it started. She asked me to help her run it and be a regular speaker. I was not comfortable giving speeches, but I believed in this program. My patients needed it, and most patients and families knew me already. So I pushed myself to rehearse to learn how to speak and lead. It was difficult. It required stepping up and being brave. I was being challenged to push past my fears and not run. My compassion for my patients outweighed my fears, so I did it. It was very popular. We ran it repeatedly throughout the years. Little did I know that I would come to be a regular speaker on other platforms in the future.

Hospice and Private Practice—More Questions

I left the hospital and joined our local hospice full-time. I also started a private practice in bereavement counseling. During this time, I developed community grief classes and an ongoing spouse bereavement group after the deaths of my own patients. Why did I do that? I needed to understand why some survivors coped better than others. I got some answers when some survivors reflected back on how it ended up working out for the better over time. For example, some people found their voices to advocate and to give back to help others. Some remarried. Some felt wiser now and chose a different partner than they chose before. Some children did better, and other children needed help. I was better prepared to help them because I knew their situations intimately through these classes and groups.

In 1984, as I was leaving the hospital to do full-time hospice, I presented at the International Hospice Symposium on childhood grief, a new idea at the time. I taught other professionals about how children grieve, the signs of unresolved grief, and how to treat them. If we were to prevent future mental health problems in adults, we needed to resolve the traumas they may have had as children. I knew, before the idea became popular, that the root of adult mental health problems was most often unresolved trauma in childhood. Most colleagues didn't seem to know this at that time and challenged me, but I was firm about this truth.

My private practice grew quickly. As people learned how to grieve, other past traumas started to surface, especially childhood traumas. Fresh grief can trigger old unresolved grief. I began to find untreated childhood abuse in many of the clients. I remembered my training in Child Protective Services and how we were able to intervene in child abuse situations so that we might be able to prevent adult mental health problems later. The country was in a major mental health awareness transition in the late eighties. People were discovering through self-help programs like Adult Children of Alcoholics and the John Bradshaw TV seminars that they could work on their own recovery. They were piecing together that their current mental health problems were possibly because of earlier traumas. People saw that the mental health community at that time tended to give drugs but didn't explore the underlying traumas.

The Clinic Years

My practice continued to grow, so I took on a business partner, Pamela DeVries Grzech, MSW, a child therapist. Before too long we founded a clinic together. We dreamed of reaching even those who could not pay, bypassing the substandard Medicaid/community mental health agency care. Insurances were changing their practices. This was the beginning of managed care, where insurance companies asked many questions about the client to grant more sessions. The clients who were coming to me really didn't fit this new model of short-term treatment. They were uncovering old traumas and needed the time, mental space, and support to deal with these old issues. We knew they could actually resolve the old and new traumas if given the time to work on them. If they resolved them, we could potentially prevent the next generation from the impact of having to endure their parents' unresolved mental health problems.

In late 1988, the Pan Am 103 airline bombing took place over Lockerbie, Scotland. A family member of a victim became my client. Suddenly I was involved with the U.S. State Department. I consulted with my contacts at the Harvard Omega Project, gave talks to the Pan Am 103 family groups in Boston and New Jersey, and helped them process their grief. The families pushed Congress and President Clinton to get answers and justice. I also discovered that two professor friends at my undergraduate college lost their college daughter in the bombing. This really brought home the disaster for me. My old, close college community was grieving. Meanwhile, more and more unresolved complex trauma was surfacing now in my practice. As I gave my clients the time they needed to work with me, more traumas were uncovered and many were permanently resolved! I had to learn as much as I could in a field that didn't understand disaster mental health or complex trauma yet.

My business partner and I employed six therapists with a consulting psychiatrist. I became clinical director and Pam, administrative director, over our W-2 employees. We didn't employ contractors because we wanted to ensure treatment excellence by supervising them with our high standards of care. Both of us continued in our previous roles as active therapists. As managed care took over the field of mental health work, we converted the clinic to a nonprofit to raise funds for those who could not pay out-of-pocket for extended services. Our clinic became very well-known regionally with radio advertising. We both became frequent guests on a southeast Michigan radio talk show and a local television show. Pam was particularly involved with local public television, providing full-length programs to parents on common topics such as "time out" and other parenting issues. Her shows drew record-high viewership.

Solving Puzzles and Using Music in My Work

I am a very curious person. I want to know what causes a presenting behavior. I always want to get to the bottom of it if a client wants to go there. I had already gained a reputation that if a client wanted to really work to get to the root of whatever was bothering them, no matter what it was, I would go with them. It usually meant that their insurance might run out. But for many clients, it didn't seem to matter. Some even remortgaged their homes or found other means of support. For others, I reduced my fee or tapped our pool of donated funds. They were tired of going from one therapist to another and not getting to the bottom of what was wrong. Therefore, I usually got clients who were ready to work, despite their fears.

I love solving puzzles. My favorite puzzle is the cryptogram —you know, those ones where the puzzle-maker hides words or text of a popular saying with encryption by replacing original letters with other letters, numbers, and symbols through substitution. I can sit for hours trying to figure out the original saying encrypted in that jumbled set of letters. I do the same with client work. I love solving the puzzle of how my clients got here in their lives, and what is behind their presenting symptoms, no matter how painful it may be. I decode the encryption that the client is presenting to me. I incorporate this puzzle-solving ability with my music and psychiatric music therapy skill sets and my other psychological training. I am a singer, highly skilled with vocal production, breathing, interpretation of song texts in different languages, and body movements when I perform. When I *hear* my clients talk, I am listening for voice inflection, pitch variations, breathing, pacing of their words, sentences, and thoughts, and the general *feel* of their emotions. Is the sound filled with anxiety? Are there surges in the emotion or breath? Is there confidence when they speak? Is there an emphasis on certain words and phrases? I also hear differences in dialect from different parts of the U.S., plus other nationalities and languages. I watch their body language, their posturing, how and when they use their arms and legs, their lips, facial expressions, wrinkles on the face and brow showing me more frequent emotional expressions, when smiles occur, their eyes—when and how they focus or don't focus, or any furtive eye movements. I observe clothing styles and how kempt they are, personal hygiene like nail beds, how they keep their hair, where they sit in my room, the pace of moving into my room, how they sit, and so on. Rhythmic movements. Breathing. Pitch. Pacing. Emotions. And, of course, I listen to their actual story. All these observations help me pace my movements and the delivery of my words as well.

For clients who are dissociative, I will move in tandem with their body movements, mirroring their movements, and reflecting sound at times, to eventually help regulate their emotions, to ground them, and connect with them on a visceral and emotional level. This creates a feeling of safety and bonding between me and my client. I ask myself how that client developed those behaviors and why. What shaped them over time? How did they arrive at a place of some kind of safety using those behaviors? What are they protecting themselves from? I am automatically observing the client's every move throughout our session.

A Major Turning Point and Revelation

By 1991, I was dealing with many complex trauma cases. During one week in April, an unusual thing happened. Four of my clients suddenly went into crisis. Each client had already been coming for several years for diagnoses that seemed to be resolved earlier in our work together. But each had wanted to continue with me because they felt there was something else lingering in their minds that we had not reached.

The first client that week had already been coming for over four years. One day, she came in mute. Unable to speak, she drew pictures of what had happened to her. As her story unfolded and she was able to speak again, it was nothing less than totally shocking to me, something about the occult and spiritual traumas. I had no idea what she was talking about. I just knew it sounded horrible. The other three clients continued to be in crisis, but we could not together figure out what was upsetting them.

The mute client caused me to wonder that week if I should ask my other three clients about the occult. No one in grad school ever taught us to ask this question. I reasoned that it couldn't hurt to ask. So, I asked. The first one let out a shriek, looked me straight in the eye, yelled, "Why did you ask me that?" and proceeded to pace around my room getting increasingly upset. She couldn't calm down. The second client got up, took something sitting on my coffee table, and started to throw it, but caught herself. She moved to the corner of my room and slid down my wall to the floor, looked at me, and let out uncontrollable, loud sobbing. The third client buried herself into the corner of my sofa under a mass of pillows and started to whimper like a child. Finally, she quietly said, "I can't do this! I can't do this."

That week I was in shock. I thought I knew these clients; I had been working with them for years. They trusted me. But now they seemed to be falling apart—all because I asked them one simple question. The therapists in my office suite overheard some of the loud outbursts and worried for me as I left each session that first week. What in the world had I gotten into? I had no idea how my life would change from then on. The question was—did I want it to change? Could I tolerate the change?

Within a few months, a couple of other colleagues in town were also getting occult disclosures from their clients. One day I received a call from the University of Michigan psych emergency room asking if I would take a client referral. This client's story sounded similar to the four clients I already had. I said, "Ah, sure. I will take them," not really knowing what I was getting into. I thought I was up for the challenge. Within a few months, I received four more similar client referrals from other therapists in my region. Word had gotten out somehow that, apparently, I knew what I was doing with victims of occult abuse, so others asked me to take their clients.

None of these nine clients knew each other. They had grown up in different areas of the U.S., and all were struggling with severe early childhood traumas. All presented in similar but unusual ways. As they would share, each often descended into trance-like states, used child-like voices, had differences in voice inflections and mannerisms from session to session, and had major lapses in memory of events that had occurred in their lives even in the last few hours or days. Some reported activities they had done in the middle of the night, like eating whole bags of cookies or chocolates, finding evidence of it with empty wrappers in the morning, but having no memory of that activity. All presented with serious trauma symptoms—nightmares, flashbacks, night sweats, the feeling of going away in their minds or 'spacing out,' and intense anxiety and panic when starting to remember horrible events. In my sixteen years of work, I had never seen these kinds of presentations in a single client before, never mind in nine of my clients.

Out of the blue, an OB-GYN physician friend of mine called. Prior to this time, I had been sharing with her about these clients and how I had no idea how to help them. That day on the phone she began the conversation with "I have one, Eileen ... I just came from their physical exam." I could hear her swallow hard; she struggled to speak but couldn't. Finally, she said, "I can't say." There was a long pause. "Eileen, you have to take them." Her patient's internal exam showed signs of being freshly abused in unusual ways.

I said, "No! It can't still be happening!" Suddenly I realized that there were perpetrators out there still doing these things and that my clients might still be at risk right now! My world turned upside down! I felt physically sick. She asked me again if I would take her patient. "Okay."

Within seven months, I had four existing clients and six new clients all reporting similar stories and behaviors. What I didn't understand at that time was that all of them also had dissociative identity disorder, previously called multiple personality disorder. I hadn't worked with that disorder but knew about it. I learned that in addition to occult-based trauma, I was dealing with trafficking survivors. All had been ritually abused in either family groups or within organized abuse groups. All had been mind-controlled by their perpetrators to keep them controlled and exploitable. These clients were essentially programmed to be slaves of the perpetrators.

What is the relationship between being a trafficking or ritual abuse survivor and having dissociative identity disorder? When little children are swept up into these organized abusive groups, the perpetrators want to make sure that the children will be faithful and loyal to the group or cult. If they traumatically abuse children during the early stages of development, their minds will split into personality parts, an automatic coping mechanism built into a young child's neurology. In certain perpetrating groups, this splitting is intentional and systematic. All of this is, of course, unbelievably horrible, and I had a hard time adjusting to this new reality. With time and treatment, however, I found that people can heal from the effects of this kind of abuse and go on to lead good and happy lives. Later, they often want to give back to help other survivors.

Throwing Out a Wider Net for Help and Education

Over the next couple of years, I was eager to learn effective treatment approaches for these extraordinarily abused clients. I scoured the Ann Arbor area, where there are over 900 therapists regularly in practice. No one knew more than I did. I reached out to southeast Michigan and found a study group an hour away with psychiatrists, psychologists, and social work psychotherapists who were also treating these kinds of clients.

We were about twenty, all gathered around a couple of large tables pulled together so we were able to share with the whole group. Each of them had only one, maybe two, clients they were seeing. I had ten! Despite the study group, it became clear after another year that I was really no further along in my understanding of how to treat these people.

My business partner, Pam, also discovered that one of her child clients seemed like she was currently being abused in similar ways. The little girl was acting out in her play what was happening to her. Pam said it was horrible. She tried to report this case to the authorities, but she got no help. She sensed there was pushback, perhaps some corruption preventing her from making any progress in the case.

In desperation and boldness, I found any and all books on the subject and hunted for how to contact those authors who knew anything about what my clients were dealing with. Eventually, I was able to find and learn from the best clinicians and researchers out there. They were very kind and spent time on the phone with me, and occasionally met me at conferences where they were presenting. I didn't want to believe that trafficking, ritual abuse, mind control, and organized abuse were actually happening. I never learned about it in grad school, but I certainly saw some evidence when I was a grad student at the Forensic Center. Those men could have been capable of abuse like this. So, I went to the police. I asked them to show me crime videos, evidence that this kind of abuse was happening, and is happening now. They did. After watching graphic evidence, I went into a crisis. It was like someone had thrown me against the wall. These clients were trying to tell me all along that indeed they had been victimized like this. And some of them feared reprisal for breathing a word of it to me. I felt like quitting, shutting down my practice. But these clients were depending on me. I couldn't just quit seeing them. What had I gotten into? I felt that if God was calling me to do this work, then somehow there was a way to deal with it. I needed to move beyond my own bystander PTSD so that my heart would be willing and soft.

I yelled to the heavens, "You've got to help me!"

Help Arrives

Wait a second! Suddenly I remembered the book by Dr. Bernice Catherine Harper—*Death: The Coping Mechanism of the Health Care Professional*—that really helped me cope when I was working with the dying earlier in my career. It felt like my prayer was answered. Back then, I had been desperate and in secondary PTSD. I was there again. I had loved my work back then. I eventually became successful and able to give back, not only to those patients but to many other professionals as they learned from me. Now I realized all over again that I either had to learn how to grieve what had happened to these current clients, or I would have to leave this area of the field. I was beginning to love my abuse survivors. But I was also dying inside. Again, there was a regular assault on my senses from hearing the horrible stories.

I was reminded, though, that if I could effectively deal with that many deaths per month when I was working in oncology and hospice—people who had no more chances to live life—then I could certainly deal with these current clients who are still alive, who still want to live life, and who are fighting to recover. So I started to grieve—hard. My shock feelings converted to grief. These were horrid stories. Stories of child trafficking even on an international scale, ritual abuse with occult themes, families and groups who did terrible things to children, and very consistent themes of spiritual abuse. I started to cry a little with my clients. Most of them had never had anyone cry for them. My heart just repelled the idea of what had happened to my clients. As I personally grieved, my heart began to touch their pain. I became more present and authentic. I also got in touch with my anger toward their perpetrators and what they had done to my clients.

One day I found that the tenth client who had come into my care was being abused so much that I just couldn't keep her safe. No matter what I tried to do, I couldn't help her. Her perpetrators consistently tricked her into going with them. Finally, I called a police investigator in another state who was familiar with these cases to possibly help this client go underground somewhere, with a different identity. I had heard of doing this before. He worked surreptitiously. He heard my request, got off the phone, and called me back from another phone number. This time he only recited a phone number. His behavior startled me, that indeed I was dealing with someone who regularly handled what seemed like an undercover operation. I called the number and got an organization in another state. They didn't identify themselves but recognized the investigator's name so they were willing to talk with me.

Linking Up with Other National Efforts

Their organization was deeply involved in caring for these survivors, advocating for them, providing resources, and educating the community and churches to help. Before I was able to put my client in contact with the organization, she disappeared. I never saw her again. This catalyzed my business partner and me to join the organization and help, which pushed us onto the national stage. We spoke at survivor conferences with this group, taught police, aligned with other therapists, attorneys, investigators, and medical professionals much more senior in this niche field and learned from them. We engaged churches to help and taught them the basics of providing protection and shelter for these survivors. We networked with many spiritual leaders nationally who had cases like this in their congregations and ministries. This organization had designed a safehouse concept for survivors that housed survivors on occult holiday nights for protection. We decided to bring that concept to Michigan and gathered a team of volunteers that ran a safehouse for almost three years. We also worked intensively with a Michigan-wide team of therapy and law professionals along with two legislators to craft legislation to convict these kinds of criminals. (Michigan is a border state with trafficking issues. Though the legislative bill failed, several years later a new Michigan governor signed three other bills that covered the points of our bill.) Eventually we left that organization to take advantage of other opportunities to serve this population.

Launching Out on My Own

In the fall of 1997, I spoke at the American Association of Christian Counselors World Congress on the complex trauma of ritual and organized abuse, which includes trafficking. I had been speaking before many audiences by then, but this audience was different. They were mental health professionals who were also spiritually based. They knew that this population also struggled with spiritual abuse, a concept that we were just beginning to understand. Most therapists know that many people have a spiritual base and that their beliefs must be acknowledged in therapy.

Many ordinary people have been both physically and spiritually abused. If the abuse takes place in what would normally be a spiritually safe and holy environment, by people you would normally trust in those environments, then it is called spiritual abuse. Spiritual abuse can take place using religious objects, inside church buildings, by clergy, by those employed in churches, and by people in the congregation of said churches. Some good ministries try to minister to these spiritually abused people, but some spiritually abused people may have also sustained occult, ritual, and organized abuse. Often people ministering to them expect that particularly wounded people will benefit from their approaches. Most are uninformed that people who have been subjected to occult or ritual abuse might be triggered by almost any good spiritual approach.

Here are the reasons. The occult or organized perpetrating group often mimics real church ceremonies and even pretends to be "prayer warriors," in the way that some good churches define that term. They may dress up as priests, ministers, and other spiritual leaders and perform abusive acts on these survivors. Or worse, they may be double agents—some real priests and spiritual leaders who are also members of these abusive groups. Clients report that these groups involve dark spiritual forces as they inflict particularly violent and extreme forms of spiritual, sexual, and physical abuse on their victims. Every effort is made to confuse the survivor in an effort to get them to repel normal spiritual approaches and church ceremonies. These perpetrators know that good spiritual approaches by safe ministers, priests, and others who are well-trained in this population will often help survivors get spiritually and physically free from these controlling groups over time. There is no way that these controlling groups want to risk losing one of their mind-controlled slaves.

Eileen Aveni, LCSW, LMSW, ACSW, BCD

Addressing the Spiritual in Therapy and in Ourselves

Besides being physical/mortal beings, I believe, we are also spiritual beings. I learned this early at the bedside of my terminal patients. We want to believe that our lives mean something while we are here. Most of the medical patients I worked with early in my terminal care years struggled with the idea of an afterlife. In life and death crises, people may seek out different spiritual practices in order to somehow connect with the transcendent: divinity or God or however they define it. These practices may not follow a specific religion, but many of us search for something beyond ourselves in life, especially when it comes to facing death.

As I work with clients, I address the spiritual, however they may define it for themselves. Our profession is remiss in not addressing spiritual issues. Many clients were abused by spiritual people, or in situations that defiled their spiritual senses. Some were even abused by perpetrators who attempted to ensure that the survivor would never gravitate to the spiritual for help. Some perpetrators even push them to shun goodness in spirituality. Clients can become confused and need help to untwist the lies, unholy teachings, and practices that were drummed into them by perpetrator leaders, involved family members, and others in the group. Clients have told me that their particular recovery path needs to address these issues. It seems that the perpetrators must have known that good spirituality can give strength, purpose, and the drive toward freedom and wholeness. Survivors often figure that out and gravitate in the opposite direction, toward goodness, and away from the toxicity of their abusers. Their abusers inadvertently push their victims toward what will free many of them.

I found that there is spiritual pushback as a therapist who

is treating spiritual abuse survivors. Because it is abuse of a spiritual nature to tamper with the spirituality of a person, it is fair to say that spiritual abuse is rooted in evil. I noticed over time that the spiritual toxicity of these stories was affecting me spiritually as well as emotionally. Not only did I need to grieve their stories, but I somehow needed to protect myself from this constant infusion of evil into my mind. I again cried out to God for an answer. I was answered in the form of a prayer.

Shortly after my desperate plea, a friend gave me a long prayer. It was surprisingly thorough in how it addressed exactly what many of my survivor clients dealt with in their spiritual abuse. It is a prayer for binding the spiritual forces that come against me daily in my work and sending them back either to where they came from or to God, whom I believe can deal with them better than I can. These spiritual forces aren't at all shy about affecting anything in my life if I let them—anything to take me down and prevent me from reaching these survivors and helping make them whole again. My husband and I use this prayer nightly. It has made a significant difference in my ability to constantly deal with the evil I hear about daily. It's like having a sword and shield to battle the forces of evil, to push them back, and to be protected from them. It is empowering and completely effective for me. (See Appendix C, p. 232.)

Going beyond Ourselves and on to What Matters in Life

The combination of grieving and doing spiritual battle against these evil forces changed me in incredibly positive ways. This combination protected me and has kept me surprisingly soft and giving in all aspects of my life. I am able to see beyond myself and my reactions. I can see who these survivors really are in their spiritual essence as well.

I came to have gentleness in my spirit and compassion toward myself, to see I was doing the best I could. I started to see these people as brave, as heroes. They had come up against evil. They were standing up to evil. They were fighting back. I wanted to stand up and cheer for them! They had come to understand the goodness of God, the divine, because they saw the polar opposite in their abusers. It was plainly evident to them that there was a spiritual force greater than themselves. Many have witnessed God or "good angels" rescuing them time after time. They've told me stories of how they also rescued others. They saw how their abusers were afraid of that goodness in those survivors, afraid of God as some would say.

Now I sit at their feet and learn from their wisdom, their intimate experience with God, and their spiritual journey. I always feel like I'm in the presence of saints when I even think about them. I admire these people for being able to survive this kind of abuse and come out strong and good despite the ways they were so horribly treated. They were taught to think badly and think in illogical and irrational ways. Instead, they came out knowing the truth, something the perpetrators didn't want. The core of the human spirit always has the potential to be centered in the truth of divinity, of goodness. When we truly examine ourselves and what is important in life, we can always come back to goodness, faithfulness, pure love, and consistent truth.

References

Harper, Bernice C. 1977. *Death: The Coping Mechanism of the Health Care Professional.* Lakeland, FL: Southeastern University Press.

Acknowledgments

This anthology would not exist were it not for the authors who wrote from their hearts and minds such wisdom around healing trauma. I am grateful to each and every one for saying yes and being patient with me as I navigated my first anthology.

I'd like to send a special shout-out to Acorn Publishing, whom I encountered at the Kauai Writers Conference. Thank you to Holly Kammier and Jessica Hammett who helped guide this book to life after some false starts. I'm so grateful for your belief in this book and skillful guidance.

My circle of friends and family have lent their ears, eyes, and support throughout this lengthy project. They include my intrepid Millennial/Gen Z cusp daughters, Maya and Larissa (the latter also agreed to be my co-editor and has better eyesight for commas and periods than I, as well as an abundance of writing talent—thanks, Larissa!), Tim Mariels, LPC, a gifted counselor and one of the few men I trust fully as a clinician and a human being, and Ericha Scott, PhD, who has been an invaluable sounding board and peer support; her knowledge is vast and boundless. Brooke Chamberlain has lent her many talents as well as her friendship to this project, including her ability to actually get me to look good in a photo. Jodi has been an endless cheerleader and "quicker picker-upper" when I navigate periods of self-doubt. I also want to thank my ex-husband, Peter Banitt, MD, for always encouraging my vision of writing and healing the world and who continues to graciously give his financial support.

Two organizations deserve mention for giving me the platform, support, and the amazing peer group of women necessary to create this book. The first is the professional organization, the International Society for the Study of Trauma and Dissociation (https://isstdworld.isst-d.org), notable for being the first (and only, I believe) international trauma organization to have a special interest group (SIG) for Ritual Abuse and Mind Control, founded by the incomparable trauma therapist and expert Ellen Lacter, PhD (https://endritualabuse.org). This SIG is now known as Organized and Extreme Abuse (OEA) and continues to educate and support clinicians who find themselves with victims of these types of horrific abuse in their practices. Three of the six authors in *Women Therapists on Healing* who have affiliation with the ISSTD are past officeholders.

The other organization is a unique peer-led group supporting people with dissociative identity disorder and the clinicians who work with them: they are An Infinite Mind (AIM, www.aninfinitemind.org). Their stated intention is "to offer a trustworthy, joyful space to connect with survivors, supporters, and clinicians." Jaime Pollack, the founder, found me and invited me to speak in the second year of their annual conference, Healing Together, that has now been running for over a decade. She has always been a warm and inviting presence with a singular focus on support for the DID and plural communities, especially in a time when there was no visibility or peer support for people with dissociative disorders and/or plural identities. Thank you, Jaime, for all you do to bring people together and support us!

I want to acknowledge and thank all of my clients over the years who have worked so hard to overcome so much adversity and taught me much about what is achievable in healing for human beings as well as the constant possibility of resilience in the face of evil. These patients of diverse backgrounds have bared their souls and challenged me to think more broadly about ethnicity and gender, among other factors, in healing from trauma. One cannot do this work without much training and psychological support, and so I would like to honor the myriad of therapists and supervisors with whom I have worked over my five decades in human services work—all but two of whom were women.

Lastly, I want to thank that one reviewer on Amazon, "Smarti," a trauma counselor who gave me a one-star review for my last book because it wasn't intersectional. They were absolutely correct. I hope they find this one to be more representational and inclusive.

Appendix A

Practical Tips for the Therapist Preparing to Work with Complex Trauma, Cults, Ritual Abuse, Mind Control, Trafficking, or Other More Difficult Work

Eileen Aveni, LCSW, LMSW, ACSW, BCD

All your life's experiences will be used to prepare you for this work, personal and job-related. Be particularly attentive to how your experiences teach you wisdom and push you to cope with pain more effectively in yourself or in others. Your heart has to stretch beyond what you will ever think it could to be able to move beyond yourself and into compassion. Don't be afraid to face hard things in life. Assess the tools you have already been given to handle these things. Ask for more tools. If you have not arrived at compassion and the ability to stay soft, then you must do the work of grieving and seeking out the spiritual in your life. The toxicity you may be exposed to in your work or in your personal life leaves a residue. It must be cleaned out to become fresh and new again.

Find what you love to do and go do that! Don't settle for less. Once you learn a particular area of treatment, make sure it continues to spark your creativity and strong interest. You could settle in and keep the status quo if you choose to. Sometimes in life that is important, especially if you have other areas of life that require more of your attention at certain times.

Don't let go of what you might be destined to do. Once you are freer to go back to what really drives you and interests you, find a way to learn more, and maybe branch out to other avenues of care. Learn how others cope or don't cope. Learn from them along the way. Glean wisdom from your observations.

Don't settle for practicing only short-term treatment techniques. Most graduate schools nowadays promote short-term treatment. There are many long-term treatment techniques that give so much reward to the therapist and are often better suited to the client's issues. Doing longer-term treatment takes you into a realm within yourself where you will be tried and tested, sometimes beyond where you thought you would be comfortable going. But the rewards are so much greater. You may have to seek out some supervision to learn longer-term treatment if you didn't learn it in grad school. Consider doing that.

You need to find the right people to talk to, get support from, and learn from. (At first, I had to seek them out with no internet!). You need to be persistent.

If you have creative outlets that give you joy, do them. I love music of any kind. I love to make music. A therapist friend of mine loves to make pottery. Another loves to make art. Finding natural outlets for creative expression will keep you balanced.

Finally, don't be afraid to teach once you learn more. Others will want to learn from you. Don't underestimate what you know. But make sure you also give your compassion and love to other clinicians. They need to know that they won't die from enduring too much secondary PTSD. Teach them how to get through it. Eventually they will get more comfortable with the work if it is their calling at that time in their lives. All of us need each other to grow into truly authentic human beings so we can continue to be there for each other.

Appendix B

For Survivors of Complex Trauma: Encouraging Words and Tips

Eileen Aveni, LCSW, LMSW, ACSW, BCD

You often struggle to be believed. That is another trauma for you, on top of going through the actual traumatic events of your life. Most of the time you probably prefer to never, ever talk about your trauma to anyone, including most therapists, because most of the time people find it hard to imagine that kind of horrible abuse actually happens. So you remain in your own pain, always crying out in your soul for some relief.

I want to suggest that you try opening up at least a little to someone, including to a good therapist. Look for someone who seems like they may have some compassion and feels safe to you. You may not be able to tell your whole story but even skimming off some pain a little at a time can help.

If you look for a therapist, ask them if they work with "complex trauma" survivors. If they don't, I would look elsewhere. A complex trauma therapist has determined for themselves that they are willing to hear hard things. They have some tools and hopefully a big heart to sit with you and listen. Go slowly with revealing what has happened to you. You probably will go slowly anyway since most perpetrators threaten their victims if they tell. So it may be built into you that you are not supposed to tell. Build that relationship with a therapist. See what they are made of. Will they cope with hard things that they hear? Or will they transfer you to someone else once they realize they don't know what to do? It really doesn't matter if they know what to do. Just being patient and being there for you can be enough. Encourage them that it's really helpful that they are able to listen. The two of you are expressing courage to each other.

Many survivors cannot afford long-term treatment or don't have good insurance. If that is the case, you may have to be creative. Many therapists will do some pro bono work with clients, that is, charge less, or even take a couple of clients for a very low fee. Try to negotiate with the therapist on a fee that you can regularly manage if you saw the therapist one to two times per week. If you think you can only afford once or twice a month, that is not advisable. Consider asking others you know if they might provide a portion of the fee so that you can go more often. Many churches and some organizations have money in their budgets to help people. Try asking them what they can do to help you. Most often you don't have to go to their church to get their help. Your mental health is worth it. You are worth it. So ask.

There are some resources out there when you cannot find a therapist who does complex trauma, or you cannot afford to engage a therapist to do some long-term work with you. Look for books on complex trauma, ritual abuse, mind control, trafficking, or organized abuse. But be careful. It can be helpful to read about these things, but you want your own memories, not someone else's memories. So be careful that books don't influence your own memories. I usually ask my clients to refrain from reading other survivor's stories until much later in their treatment after they have established many of their memories.

But some books are designed as self-help manuals. You might try one of those kinds of books.

The most important thing I can say to you is: You really are amazing! You not only survived horrible things, but you are now in the process of recovery. I am so proud of you! You are inspiring to me. The very fact that you are here reading this is because you have a kind of resiliency that few of us will ever have. You know that you lived through something really hard. Many of us will never really understand what that was like. I can never walk in your shoes. But I can walk with you as you step into your calling.

Perpetrators didn't want you to discover that in yourself because they might lose control of you. You might come to know truth, goodness, and get empowered to move beyond their control. Well, doesn't that tell you that whatever they wanted was what you don't want for your life now? Keep moving ahead. Your life belongs to you. Take it back!

Appendix C

Christian Prayers for Protection and Healing

Eileen Aveni, LCSW, LMSW, ACSW, BCD

This entire prayer can be prayed for oneself or for others—all at once.

A Binding Prayer for Protection

In the name of Jesus Christ, by the power of his cross and blood, we bind the spirits, powers, and forces of the enemy. We command anything that is not of the Kingdom of God to depart now, never to return.

In Jesus's name, we bind all interplay, interaction, and communication of unclean or evil spirits as it affects us and our ministry.

In Jesus's name, we break any curses, hexes, spells, or assignments sent against us (them) and send them directly to Jesus for him to deal with as he will. Lord, we ask you to send your Holy Spirit now to fill us and this place. Come, Holy Spirit, Come.

We claim the protection of the shed blood of Jesus Christ

over _____ (list people and situations that need protection and prayer).

Thank you for your protection, Lord. Amen.

Jesus, thank you for sharing with us your wonderful ministry of healing and deliverance. Thank you for the healings that we have seen and experienced today.

We realize that the sickness and evil we encounter is more than our humanity can bear, so cleanse us of any sadness, negativity, anxiety, or despair that we may have picked up.

If our ministry has tempted us to anger, impatience, passivity, lust, anxiety, unbelief, or pride, cleanse us of those temptations and replace them with love, joy, peace, patience, kindness, goodness, faithfulness, gentleness, self-control, wisdom, repentance, forgiveness, purity, trust, perseverance, courage, fearless leadership, humility, hope, faith, and thanksgiving.

If any evil spirits have attached themselves to us or oppress us in any way, we command them, spirits of earth, air, fire or water, of the netherworld, of nature, of death, or of any other sort, in the name of Jesus, by the power of his cross and blood, to depart—now—and go straight to Jesus for him to deal with as he will.

Come, Holy Spirit, renew us; fill us anew with your power, your life, and your joy. Strengthen us where we have felt weak and clothe us with your light. Fill us with life.

Lord Jesus, please send your Holy angels to minister to us and our families—guard us and protect us from all sickness, harm, and accidents. Give us safe travels.

We praise You now and forever, Father, Son, and Holy Spirit, and we ask these things in Jesus's Holy Name that He may be glorified. Amen.

(Adapted from Christian Healing Ministries, Jacksonville, Florida, 904-765-3332)

Glossary

Affect
A clinical/therapy word for emotion and feelings.

Ajaw/Ahaw
Means "lord" in several Mayan languages. For many Maya, Ajaw is also the fundamental principle of time and space. In Urdu, Ajaw means "all in one."

Alloparented
Describes children raised by someone who is not their direct parent, such as a grandparent.

Brainstem
At the base of the back of the brain, connecting the spinal cord to the cerebellum, it is responsible for basic involuntary functions of the body: sleep cycles, body temperature, breathing, blood pressure, heart rate, consciousness, and more.

B&D or S&M
Sexual play and preferences that include bondage and domination (B&D) or sadism and masochism (S&M). Practitioners need education to perform these preferences safely and have systems in place to maintain consent throughout, such as using a "safe word" to slow down or stop the interaction.

Bricoleur
One who makes bricolage, a piecemeal construction of an object, often artistic in nature.

Central nervous system
The brain, spinal cord, and cerebellum.

Codependent
Describes a person who compulsively caretakes people and seeks out people for relationships who need their help. This person often has low self-esteem and can suffer from "relationship addiction." It is a learned behavior that can be transmitted generationally. This word came out of addiction treatment when it was noted that addicts often had people in their lives who would "enable" them to continue their addiction by doing for them what they should do for themselves.

Collective psyche
Sets of psychic constructs, perceptions, and thoughts that are shared by large groups of people such as states, nations, corporations, or the world. This idea arises out of Carl Jung's idea of the "collective unconscious," a substrate of archetypes and ideas widely but unconsciously shared across cultures and humanity.

Default mode network
A term from neuroscience to describe the activity of a brain in a state of rest, which can include daydreaming, internal dialogue, memory, theory of one's own mind and others' minds, and introspection. It is deactivated when the brain is in external work mode.

Dissociative identity disorder (DID)
A recognized mental health disorder in the *DSM* and *ICD-10* involving the formation of two or more distinct identities—also called parts, alters, or headmates—within an individual. These identities can be overt or covert, active or dormant.

Dopamine
A brain neurotransmitter involved in feelings of pleasure and reward. Low dopamine can be associated with problems such as Parkinson's disease and major depressive disorder.

Dopaminergic response
The body's system to produce, secrete, and distribute dopamine.

Emic
An adjective that means to consider a language or culture from that culture's point of view; a way of engaging with others that the National Association of Social Workers calls "cultural humility."

Emotional unit
A group of people who are deeply emotionally connected to each other, such as a family, whose psychology cannot be fully understood without understanding the group that they are a part of.

Endogenous opioid system

The pain-relieving system of the mind/body mechanism consisting of three different kinds of opioids made within the body that decrease pain and increase pleasure as neurotransmitters throughout the brain.

Ehlers-Danlos syndrome

A group of connective tissue disorders characterized by hypermobile joints, frequent subluxations, abnormal scar formation, and stretchy skin or other tissues in the body. Symptoms can range from mild to life-threatening and can show up in systems throughout the body.

Environmental trauma

The emotional, physical, or psychological response to an event, natural environment, natural disaster, community environment, or series of events that has lasting negative effects on an individual's functioning.

Family constellations work

A technique for healing that involves a re-creation of the family dynamic through poses and embodying the energy of the family by workshop participants. People have found unexpectedly powerful healings in this unusual modality created by Burt Hellinger in Germany.

Family projection process

As described by Murray Bowen, the renowned family therapy pioneer, the parent(s) project their issues onto their child(ren), who then accept and embody that projection.

Family systems theory
Describes the healthy or unhealthy dynamics between family members and how the system of the family tends to return to homeostasis in either a functional or dysfunctional way.

Feldenkrais
Created by Moshe Feldenkrais to develop more ease and less pain and stiffness in the body through exercises and paying attention to patterns in the body that may reflect relationships and events.

Griots
West African storytellers in the native tradition, narrators of oral traditions, poetry, history, and genealogy.

Intersectional feminism
Based on the concept of "intersectionality" coined by American civil rights advocate and scholar Kimberlé Crenshaw, this feminist lens takes into account the many factors that affect women and their lack of rights and/or discrimination, such as race and sexual orientation.

Latchkey kid
A slang term in use for decades referring to preteen children who came home to an empty house and had to let themselves in with a "latchkey."

Limbic system
The middle part of the brain that is responsible for what we consider mammalian functions: emotions, behaviors, connection, socialization, etc.

Medical trauma

Defined by the International Society for Traumatic Stress Studies as a set of psychological and physiological responses to pain, injury, serious illness, medical procedures, and frightening treatment experiences.

Mestiza

A woman of mixed heritage of European ancestry with Indigenous non-European ancestry in Latin America.

Mind control programming

Intense behavioral conditioning using extreme measures over a long period of time to engineer predetermined behaviors into a person's mind, usually starting at birth or just before birth, by organized entities such as the military, organized crime, and secret government agencies. "Successful" programming turns a person into a slave without walls.

Othering

The xenophobic social and behavioral act of excluding people who are deemed to be "not like you" and treating them with condescension, discrimination, and/or suspicion.

People-please

To fawn or codependently need to make everyone happy with you and your actions.

Periaqueductal gray

A key brain structure in pain propagation and modulation, sympathetic responses, and defensive and aversive behaviors.

Positionality
Describes one's identity or position with regard to various factors such as race, ethnicity, social class, education, heritage, gender, etc.

Social constructionism
The idea that we collectively create our social reality through shared perceptions, definitions, constructs, and values, rather than there existing a de facto objective reality.

Soma
Another word for body, often used in yoga circles, when talking about the inner perception of that body. Originally a Greek word that meant body.

The Strange Situation
A set of psychological experiments designed by Mary Ainsworth in the 1970s to evaluate toddler's responses to stressful situations involving their caretakers. Modern attachment style descriptions arose out of these experiments, which demonstrated how children responded to reunions with their caretakers differently depending on their level of safe attachment to those caretakers. Some children's responses of wanting to move both toward and away from a scary caretaker were the possible etiology of dissociation.

Trauma response
The physical and emotional response of the body to terror and traumatic events.

<u>**Ventral medial prefrontal cortex (vmPFC)**</u>

The vmPFC plays an important role in regulating and inhibiting our response to emotions. The vmPFC seems to use our emotional reactions to model our behavior and control emotional reactions in certain social situations.

About the Authors and Editors

Eileen Aveni, LCSW, BCD, holds a diploma in clinical social work and specializes in treating dissociative disorders, complex trauma, ritual abuse, mind control, and spiritual abuse. She is an international speaker, supervisor, trainer, and consultant and is writing her first of several books for therapists and survivors. She developed the Migration Model, a spiritual/psychological approach to undoing mind control in ritual abuse. A professionally trained musician, she loves traveling and making music with her husband. www.ra-free.org

Larissa Miranda, BA, BSN, RN (editor), is an editor, award-winning writer, and nurse with over ten years of experience in content creation. She currently works as a hospice nurse administering care to terminally ill patients and their families. She began writing health content in 2018, and her work appears on platforms from local nonprofit blogs to national publications such as Health and WebMD. She volunteers as a crisis counselor for the Crisis Text Line and serves on the board of the Pacific Youth Choir in Portland, Oregon. When not writing about health, she likes to write about food and drink. www.larissabanitt.com

Lisa Danylchuk, LMFT, E-RYT, is a licensed psychotherapist and founder of the Center for Yoga and Trauma Recovery. A graduate of UCLA and Harvard University, she has pioneered the field of trauma-informed yoga and transformed our understanding of embodiment practices in therapeutic work. Author of three books on healing traumatic stress, she created the Yoga for Trauma Online Training Program and hosts the *How We Can Heal Podcast*, featuring interviews with leaders in trauma, dissociation, and healing. https://howwecanheal.com

Christine Forner, MSW, RSW, has over thirty-five years of experience working with individuals with traumatic dissociation. She specializes in the intersection of dissociation, mindfulness, and the role that misogyny and the patriarchy play in the origination and perpetuation of psychopathy. Christine was the president of the International Society for the Study of Trauma and Dissociation in 2019. She is the author of *Dissociation, Mindfulness, and Creative Meditations: Trauma-Informed Practices to Facilitate Growth* (Routledge, 2017).

Javelin Hardy, LMSW, was born and raised in Louisiana but has resided in Portland, Oregon, for the past thirty years. Javelin authored two books of poetry: The Girl Inside Me: For All Who Suffered Sexual Abuse or Trauma as Children (Dancing Moon Press, 2020) and It Takes a Journey to Heal (Dancing Moon Press, 2020). Understanding the traumas that have affected African families intergenerationally is her passion. She is an author, yoga instructor, certified Usui/Holy Fire Reiki III healer, and vibrational sound practitioner. www.javelinhelpsheal.com

Leann R. Johnson, MS, is an industrial-organizational psychology practitioner, a systems therapist, owner of Innovatus, LLC, and has studied at the University of Oxford (UK), receiving an executive diploma in Strategy and Innovation (2026). She has thirty years of experience as an equity and inclusion professional, having worked in nonprofit, higher education, private, and public sectors. Leann is a professional storyteller and an actor in comedic and dramatic improvisational theater in Portland, Oregon. She co-created Black Woman/White Woman, an evolving, experimental work featured in 2022 and 2025 at the National Conference on Race and Ethnicity.

Dr. Jamie Marich, LPCC-S, REAT, RYT-500 (she/they/we), travels internationally teaching on EMDR therapy, dissociation, expressive arts, and spiritual trauma, while maintaining a private practice and online training operation, the Institute for Creative Mindfulness, in Akron, Ohio (Erie Nation land). She has authored over ten books on trauma recovery, most notably *Dissociation Made Simple: A Stigma-Free Guide to Embracing Your Dissociative Mind and Navigating Life* (North Atlantic Books, 2023) and *Trauma and the 12 Steps: An Inclusive Guide for Enhancing Recovery* (North Atlantic Books, 2020). Her latest releases are *You Lied to Me About God: A Memoir* (North Atlantic Books, 2024), which received a Kirkus starred review, and she is currently under contract to write *Memoir Writing as Spiritual Practice*, due for a 2026 release. Her company Creative Mindfulness Media produced and published *Queering EMDR Therapy* (2025). www.jamiemarich.com

Susan Pease Banitt, LCSW, RYT (author and editor), is the award-winning author of *The Trauma Tool Kit: Healing from the Inside Out* (Quest, 2012) and *Wisdom, Attachment and Love in Trauma Therapy: Beyond Evidence-Based Practice* (Routledge, 2018). Susan trained in the Harvard teaching hospitals and is a pioneer in the field of complementary therapies in psychological healing. She has nearly fifty years of experience in mental health work, with specialties in PTSD, dissociative disorders, autism spectrum, and medical social work. Susan provides international consultation and supervision to mental health clinicians who seek answers to complicated cases of complex trauma and dissociation in their clients.

She has spoken nationally and internationally at conferences, retreats, medical facilities, universities, webinars, and governmental bodies as well as her own workshops and classes. Susan co-hosted on the *Rebel Justice Podcast* and is active on social media. Having retired from individual psychotherapy in 2023, she is focusing her efforts on writing and training therapists to work with extreme trauma, especially survivors of mind control, ritual, and cultic abuse. She maintains a spiritual consulting practice for people with psychic or indigenous abilities, people identifying as Lightworkers and Starseeds, and people who want to explore alternative forms of spirituality as part of their healing journey and is developing a new AI-based therapy assist app. www.suepeasebanitt.com

Hūhana Jade Barclay, MPH, MBA, is a neurodivergent, disabled Māori researcher and therapist, closing the gap between real-life complexity and siloed approaches in healthcare and research. A well-known ambassador for digital literacy, health equity, accessibility, and patient scientists, Jade works at the intersection of health, technology, policy, and social justice in Australia. Their work equips leaders to decolonize communication and practice, ensuring that diverse communities are represented wherever decisions are made—building a more inclusive and just world.

Mimi Savage, PhD, RDT/BCT, is an associate professor at the California Institute of Integral Studies (MA counseling psychology and expressive arts). Conference topics and publications include narrative, arts-based research exploring self-identity with young women adopted from foster care, and facilitating houseless women on Skid Row, LA. Clinical work consists of residential treatment centers and inpatient psychiatric units. On faculty at UCLArts and Healing SEA program, she was the North American Drama Therapy Association education chair and directs SoCal Drama Therapy Center. www.socaldramatherapycenter.com

Robin Shapiro, MSW, LICSW, has been a psychotherapist since 1981 and has expertise in EMDR, ego state, somatic, relational, attachment-focused, and many other therapies. She is skilled at synthesizing diverse therapy modalities and explaining how to use them, simply, and often entertainingly, to other therapists. Her passion is helping psychotherapists understand and effectively treat their clients. She is the author/editor of five books, all published by W. W. Norton. She lives in Seattle, Washington. www.emdrsolutions.com

Claudia Villacova, MA, LCPC, is a psycho-spiritual Medicine Wombyn who grounds her work within the Indigenous Medicine Wheel. She pulls from an ecological, phenomenological, and developmental lens to work through trauma from an embodied position and holds space for the sovereign self to emerge into self-governance with an ecological grounding. Claudia provides counseling, consulting, curriculum development, circle facilitator training, and co-leads organizational culture and relationship building for Truth, Racial Healing and Transformation (TRHT) Greater Chicago.